ROOSEVELT'S
IMAGE
BROKERS

Kennikat Press
National University Publications
Series in American Studies

General Editor
James P. Shenton
Professor of History, Columbia University

ALFRED HAWORTH JONES

ROOSEVELT'S IMAGE BROKERS

Poets, Playwrights, and the Use of the Lincoln Symbol

National University Publications
Kennikat Press ● 1974
Port Washington, N.Y. ● London

Library of Congress Catalog Card No. 74-77651
ISBN: 0-8046-9079-0

Manufactured in the United States of America

Published by
Kennikat Press Corp.
Port Washington, N.Y./London

For My Mother and Father

CONTENTS

Introduction   *3*

one   The Recovery of a Usable American Past   *7*

two   The Emergence of the Lincoln Image   *25*

three   Abe Lincoln in Illinois: Pageant and Exhortation   *38*

four   The Lincoln of Sandburg and His Admirers   *51*

five   Roosevelt: The Democratic Lincoln   *63*

six   William Allen White and an Interventionist Lincoln   *82*

seven   Two Poets and Two Presidents   *97*

eight   Conclusion   *112*

Bibliographical Note   *118*

Notes   *121*

Index   *130*

ACKNOWLEDGMENTS

This study began as a doctoral dissertation at Yale University, where Professor John Morton Blum served as its candid and discerning director. Professor Sydney E. Ahlstrom of Yale also helped refine the work in its initial stages. University of Minnesota Professors Clarke A. Chambers, David W. Noble, and Peter N. Carroll subsequently contributed valuable suggestions for revisions of the manuscript. In a *summa* thesis written under my supervision at Minnesota, Ms. Elizabeth Jane Wheeler added to my appreciation of Franklin Roosevelt's heroic dimension. Throughout, my wife Bonnie, who has her own career, followed the development of this study with abiding interest and concern. To all these individuals, and to Iowa State University for supporting the typing of the manuscript, I owe a debt of gratitude.

ROOSEVELT'S
IMAGE
BROKERS

INTRODUCTION

It has been said that in 1932 Franklin D. Roosevelt won the Presidency mainly on the strength of the fact that he was *not* Herbert Hoover. To be sure, the election hardly represented a ringing endorsement of the Democratic candidate. Whether Roosevelt could convert his victory into a personal vote of confidence remained to be seen. By 1940, when he won election to an unprecedented third term, however, the verdict was clear: Roosevelt, more than any other twentieth century President, was the people's choice. What factors had transformed the man in the White House into a veritable national hero? Among them, his use of history was important. With the aid of two poets and a playwright, the President effectively exploited parallels with the past for his own political advantage. To show how this was accomplished is the purpose of this study.

Franklin Roosevelt understood the reinforcing relationship of past and present. While attempting to renew public confidence in national institutions, he encouraged a complementary search for reassurance in the American past. While undertaking to meet the Depression crisis with a political program that embraced a majority of the people, he commended the concurrent rediscovery of a common popular heritage. In short, the national search for unity and direction during the 1930s took place simultaneously on two levels. The historical quest culminated in the emergence of the unifying and motivating image of Abraham Lincoln, symbolic of both the best in the American liberal tradition and the democratic faith.

During his second Presidential term, Franklin Roosevelt increasingly manipulated the new Lincoln image. First, he made it serve the partisan purpose of providing historical justification for New Deal policies. Then, after hostilities in Europe drew his attention from domestic affairs, the President enlisted the Lincoln image in support of a nonpartisan foreign policy of aid to the Allies.

Any study of the political uses of the Lincoln image must concentrate as much on the prophets of the parallel between past and present as on its substance. Neither the initial revitalization of the symbol of the Great Emancipator nor its identification with the programs of the Roosevelt Administration originated in Washington. Rather, they emerged primarily from the work of two poets and a playwright laboring quite independently. For all their differences, however, Carl Sandburg, Stephen Vincent Benét, and Robert E. Sherwood shared a common intellectual and ideological outlook that led them to support the Democratic President.

All three were "liberal" writers. They measured contemporary society by a conception of the national heritage which emphasized the progressive aspects of traditional values and institutions. When they found the present wanting, they lamented the unkept promise of American life and doubled their efforts to renew it. Their democratic assumptions led these writers to grant that the ultimate verdict on national affairs rested with the people. But unlike the avant-garde highbrows or the lowbrow popularizers, Sandburg, Benét, and Sherwood neither scorned the American jury nor pandered to it. Instead, they sought to educate and guide it. Indeed, the didactic element in their writing, more than anything else, won for them the condescending "middle-brow" label. Their hortatory task represented more than mere celebration, however, for the lessons of the American past were mixed. As Benét stated, "two moods"—enthusiasm and self-criticism—had been part of the American mind from the start. Ever since, "responsible" writers had maintained a critical but affirmative attitude toward their native land. In contrast to those whom Archibald MacLeish condemned in 1940 as "The Irresponsibles," these writers maintained their faith in America's ultimate possibilities.

In their rediscovery of a heroic American past, Sandburg, Benét, and Sherwood found particular inspiration in Abraham Lincoln, savior of the Union and liberator of the slaves, whom they erected into the foremost symbol of American democracy. Then, deserting their nonpartisan independence, the two poets and the playwright linked the Great Emancipator with the incumbent President, casting Franklin Roosevelt in the role of a Democratic Lincoln. Indeed, Sherwood's celebrated drama, *Abe Lincoln in Illinois,* was the pivotal factor in the crystallization of the new image.

Their interpretation of the lessons of the Civil War, as enunciated by Lincoln at Gettysburg, next led all three writers to various expressions of interventionist sentiment, often involving William Allen White's Committee to Defend America by Aiding the Allies, which became an adjunct to the Administration's bipartisan foreign policy. In the two years between the outbreak of the Second World War and Pearl Harbor, the Lincoln image became identified with aid to the victims of aggression.

Rather than first inquire into its content, the liberal middlebrow writers who employed the Lincoln image straightway exploited parallels between the experience of the Great Emancipator and his modern Democratic successor. They used the Lincoln name, whatever its previous implications, as a sanction for Administration policies and programs. Without some correspondence between historical image and political reality, of course, the device would have failed, and the authors would have discarded it. President Lyndon B. Johnson's abortive attempt, early in 1968, to invoke Lincoln's blessing upon his Vietnam policy exposed the limits of the analogy. But at the time of the Second World War the parallel proved convincing. That Roosevelt and his supporters continually summoned the Great Emancipator's name and example in behalf of their goals testified to its effectiveness. In the image of Lincoln they found a potent force for national unity and purpose in contemporary American life.

chapter one

THE RECOVERY OF A
USABLE AMERICAN PAST

1

The Great Crash marked an intellectual as well as an economic watershed in American history. With the first signs of the Depression, observers sensed a change in the national mind; the very threat of adversity awakened a new social consciousness. Even before Franklin D. Roosevelt and the New Deal threw public resources behind the enterprise, Americans began to take stock of their country. After 1933, the government-sponsored cultural projects furthered an adventure in national rediscovery which represented one of the most far-reaching developments of the Depression decade.

Manifestations of this renewed interest in America abounded: regionalism in painting and music, historical novels and films, the recovery of folklore and customs, scholarly biographies and sociological monographs, the vogue of documentary photographs and dramas, the WPA guides and historical surveys. Whatever the apparent chaos of activity, however, the overall cultural development of the decade revealed a trend. The "drive toward national inven-

7

tory," as Alfred Kazin characterized the phenomenon, "began by reporting the ravages of the depression and ended by reporting on the national inheritance." The movement was distinctly from present to past: from current affairs to history. But what did it all mean—the preservation of documents, the indexing of artifacts, the measuring of old buildings, the opening of the National Archives in 1937? To some, as Merle Curti has pointed out, it "suggested the end of an era, an effort to summarize the past, now that all the returns were in, before moving on to a new chapter." But to many others it represented, above all, a search for a usable American past, for a tradition that could provide guidance and justification for present programs and projects. In Harold Clurman's words, the Depression generation "studied our history with the purpose of shaping our future."[1]

There was of course nothing unique about the 1930s impulse to seek a usable national history. Other generations of Americans, too, had undertaken their own such quests. In the early years of the century, for example, a radical young generation of writers clamored for a redefinition of the American tradition in order to free the native artist from the crippling influence of contemporary culture. Inspired and led by Van Wyck Brooks, these Young Intellectuals condemned the useless past provided them by the academic establishment, which had canonized only those authors who accommodated themselves to the "commercial mind" of the late nineteenth century. "The present is a void," Brooks declared, "and the American writer floats in that void because the past that survives in the common mind of the present is a past without living value." An alternative, however, lay in what Brooks called a "usable past." "If . . . we cannot use the past our professors offer us, is there any reason why we should not create others of our own?"[2]

The reconstruction of history would perforce begin with Walt Whitman, who "laid the cornerstone of a national ideal capable . . . of releasing personality and of retrieving for our civilization, originally deficient in the richer juices of human nature, and still further bled and flattened out by the Machine Process, the only sort of 'place in the sun' really worth having." But the usable past must necessarily also end with Whitman. He alone among American authors could move the modern writer. The past waiting to be discovered, then, was a meager one, as Brooks conceded; what stood out were "the shortcomings, the needs, the difficulties of our literary life." But the realization that "others have desired the things we desire and have encountered the same obstacles, and that in some degree time has begun to face those obstacles down and make the way straight for us," the young critic argued, might help the creative forces in America to unite against their common reactionary enemies.[3]

Whatever their despair at the current state of literary history, Brooks and his comrades, notably Randolph Bourne, Waldo Frank, Harold Stearns, and Lewis Mumford, wrote in a time of buoyant optimism and hope. They were missionaries preaching the gospel of art, prophets pointing the way to cultural salvation. In that crusade, the use of the past was largely negative: history represented something to transcend.

Then came the First World War and the disruption of so much that had seemed to promise a new day for America. The disintegration of the anticipatory spirit of Young America can perhaps be seen in the short life of *The Seven Arts* magazine, founded in 1916 by Waldo Frank and James Oppenheim to further the Brooksian revolution: "For the first time, the aesthetic and the national . . . are joined dynamically in American literary action."[4] In the first issue, the editors proclaimed their faith "that we are living in the first days of a renascent period, a time which means for America the coming of that national self-consciousness which is the beginning of greatness." A year later, a casualty of the jingoistic reaction to its anti-interventionist sentiments, the

journal folded with a last lament for the lost "current" of
desire among American youth for art and freedom. "Across
this current, like a sudden dam, came the war. It carried with
it a menace to what we believed to be the promise of
American life."[5]

The particular search for a usable American past upon
which the Young Intellectuals had embarked was also
abandoned during the war—before, indeed, it had produced
much history. Only the movement's progenitor, Van Wyck
Brooks, continued for a time to write as though nothing had
changed. For most Americans, the Armistice ushered in a
new era and new interests. Many seemed determined to forget
the recent past, as Harding's election and the politics of
"normalcy" indicated. In times of complacency, men live
primarily in the present; and as if to emphasize their emancipation from history, the generation of the 1920s made heroes
of their contemporaries. The decade belonged to living
embodiments of their own ideal self-images—the tech-
nologists of a business civilization. That Americans so
admired Henry Ford, Herbert Hoover, and Charles Lindbergh
as to metamorphose them into icons is a commentary on the
materialism of the postwar era.

When readers during the 1920s turned to the past at all,
they sought a scapegoat. In that peculiar literary creation, the
Puritan, some writers of the time found their victim with a
vengeance. Depicted as a combination of pious religiosity and
business acumen, this personage better represented the late
nineteenth century than the first years of colonization,
Victorianism than Calvinism, Anthony Comstock than John
Winthrop. H. L. Mencken singled him out for such special
abuse that a leading cultural historian of the period has found
it "most difficult to explain. . . ."[6] Apparently, these spuri-
ous representatives of the past century stood condemned as
grandsires of the civilization from which the current generation sought to escape through ridicule or condemnation. For

the germ of this idea, writers of the 1920s unfairly cited Van Wyck Brooks. Actually, the author of *The Wine of the Puritans* (1908) had never intended to foster so jejune a past.

To an extent, the "new" biography that flourished during the postwar decade also represented a reaction against the past, precipitated perhaps by animus toward those who had led the nation into world conflict and then betrayed their countrymen's high hopes with a botched peace. It was antihistorical: psychoanalyzing or debunking the heroes of other eras, by discrediting them, only made the present loom all the larger. Apart from a sense of outrage over the mess their forebears had made of the world, however, writers of the 1920s had good reasons for abandoning the stately, sentimental tradition in Victorian biography, "the old three story gingerbread monument to a defunct reputation," as Stephen Vincent Benét affectionately described it. Its practitioners, as the biographer Claude Fuess admitted, had shown a consistent "unwillingness to expose any deceit or indiscretion in the immaculate hero." Besides a refreshing realism about their ancestors, the "modern" biographers brought some useful insights from psychology to bear upon the figures they sought to interpret. But candor could degenerate into cynicism, as in the case of Paxton Hibben's portraits of Henry Ward Beecher and William Jennings Bryan, and personality analysis into character assassination, when, for example, Abraham Lincoln became the victim of Edgar Lee Masters. Excesses in biography during the Twenties, then, paralleled those in other fields; and the inevitable reaction set in with the Depression. "Back to . . . Victorian biography," urged Bernard DeVoto in 1932. "For the great Victorians, however timorous in refusing to call fornication by a ruder name, had as biographers an invincible integrity."[7]

2

The Great Crash brought the epoch of prosperity to a sudden and dramatic close, and the Depression discredited its primary symbols. That idol, the contemporary technician with his stake in the expanding economy, collapsed along with the stock market; and the era of which he had been chief representative fell precipitously into disrepute. Indeed, the overreaction against the decade now paralleled the complacency which had accompanied the affluence: both went too far.

The new attitude of rejection encouraged some observers to view the Twenties as an exceptional interlude of irresponsibility—an aberrational interruption—separating the "normal" periods of responsible liberal reform before the War and after 1933. This notion also emboldened a number of writers to interpret the Depression-inspired revival of interest in American history, like contemporary developments in other fields, as a continuation of that which had preceded the War. A close comparison of the two movements, however, reveals the limitations of such a conception. Furthermore, the origins of both the rediscovery of America and the renewed preoccupation with the national past can be found in the same discredited decade of Ford, Lindbergh, and Hoover.

The Great Depression that settled upon the land after the Crash of 1929 touched every aspect of American life. If not the exclusive cause of the revived interest in the native history, it constituted the chief catalyst. Accordingly, in motivation the 1930s' search for a usable past bore a marked contrast to that of the prosperous prewar era. An optimistic spirit of rebellion, corresponding to the contemporaneous political reform impulse, had attended the early twentieth century concern with history. For the radical Young Intellectuals, the men and values of the late nineteenth century represented barriers to their own artistic energy and creati-

vity. The Depression generation possessed neither the im-
patience nor the self-confidence of their prewar predecessors.
In a time of insecurity, they dared not repudiate their
forebears. As John Dos Passos put it, "We need to know what
kind of firm ground other men, belonging to generations
before us, have found to stand on."[8]

Van Wyck Brooks and his apostles, filled with a sense of
confidence and ambition which reflected the climate of those
days, felt apologetic about their nation's prior cultural
achievements. To discover and illuminate the historic barriers
to innovation and accomplishment, in social life as well as
art, became one of their tasks. The uses of the past then
would be largely negative: the Young Radicals sought to
learn from the abortive experiences of their artistic fore-
fathers how to avoid compromise, frustration, and defeat in
literature. In Brooks this purpose came through in tangible
terms. Out of his contempt for the contemporary cultural
inheritance evolved the conception for a series of studies in
nineteenth century literary history which would dramatize
how American writers had been maimed in spirit by their
society. The works began to appear after the Armistice. *The
Ordeal of Mark Twain* (1920) and *The Pilgrimage of Henry
James* (1925) told complementary stories of thwarted consciousness. As the author summarized his interpretation,
"Mark Twain stayed at home and surrendered to the tastes of
his time. Henry James fled to Europe and the uprooting
withered and wasted his genius."[9] At best, however, Brooks'
reading of history, like that of the other Young Intellectuals,
was cursory—designed primarily to justify a preconceived
indictment of the present.

By contrast, the Depression generation of writers could
discover in the present no promise to use as an excuse for
condemning the past. Instead, they felt drawn toward
history—"driven," in John Dos Passos' words—"by a pressing
need to find answers to the riddles of today."[10] If they
turned to the past as a guide to the present, then the

landmarks must be accurate and reliable or the lessons would be misleading. Hence, meticulous attention to authenticity became a canon of the decade. Writers of the prewar era had well-defined goals; accordingly, they employed history selectively to vindicate their rebellion. But their counterparts twenty years later, lacking confidence in their own vision, sought an objective version of history to provide guidelines for action.

During the 1920s, two very different literary groups had anticipated and initiated the renewed consciousness of America and the affirmative uses of its past which characterized the mood of the following decade. Awareness of native themes had sprung from an unlikely source—some of the expatriate artists who settled abroad, frequently in Paris—after the Armistice. The new interest in the American past was prefigured in the work of a more conventional group. Professional historical scholars, their numbers swelled by young recruits, had undertaken two cooperative projects that helped mold the image of the past predominating after the Crash.

That literary expatriates contributed significantly to the rediscovery of America involves no paradox if the nature of the "lost generation" and the meaning of their alienation are accurately construed. If lost, many of the sensitive young writers of the 1920s felt determined to find themselves as well as solid cultural ground to stand on. Often they sought freedom abroad from the distractions of the present, the better to understand themselves and their heritage. Exile hardly represented a repudiation of their nationality—only perhaps of their countrymen. "I feel more American than I have ever felt before," wrote Louis Bromfield from Paris in 1927. "I find that all my senses, my perceptions, have become with regard to America sharpened and more highly sensitive." In 1934, after he had returned from France, Van Wyck Brooks' erstwhile colleague Harold Stearns admitted that "our participation which many people hailed as an end of our 'isolation' did in cold fact result in a greater nationalistic feeling than we had ever before known. . . ." The works which the expatriates produced abroad, as well as after their return, reflected their continuing preoccupation. According to their self-appointed historian, Malcolm Cowley, "In Paris or Pamplona, writing, drinking, watching bullfights or making love, they continued to desire a Kentucky hill cabin, a farmhouse in Iowa or Wisconsin, the Michigan woods, the blue Juniata, a country they had 'lost, ah, lost' as Thomas Wolfe kept saying; a home to which they couldn't go back."[11]

Aside from Vernon Louis Parrington's *Main Currents in American Thought*, a three-volume reinterpretation which in impulse and emphasis belonged to the Progressive Era of Charles Beard and J. Allen Smith, the two major historical achievements of the 1920s were collaborative works which pointed in the opposite direction. Scores of scholars contributed to *The Dictionary of American Biography* (20 volumes, 1928-36), while a different author was responsible for each of the twelve projected volumes of *The History of American Life* series (1928-44). As collective enterprises, these works anticipated many of the cultural projects, such as the state guides, later undertaken by the New Deal. More important, they reflected what became the dual preoccupations of historical writing during the following decade—the achievements of individual Americans, on the one hand, and of the great democratic mass on the other.

Affirmative in spirit, ambitious in conception, and inclusive in scope, the accumulating volumes of these two projects constituted a monumental rebuke to those who belittled the nation and its history. If the British had their *Dictionary of National Biography*, then Americans must have a comparable compilation. The lives of hundreds of their ancestors would be sketched in portraits which sought to combine the best of the old biography and the new. As the original editor, Allen Johnson, declared, "contributors have been urged not to rest content with a bare narrative of events, but so far as possible to leave the reader with a definite impression of the personality and achievements of the subject. . . ."[12] The work represented nothing less than a testimony to some Americans' mature sense of nationality.

While the DAB honored a small minority of the nation, Arthur M. Schlesinger's and Dixon Ryan Fox's *History of American Life* undertook to describe the common experience of the whole people. As titles like *The Rise of the Common Man* and *The Rise of the City* indicated, the authors reached well beyond the boundaries of traditional history to embrace their subject. "It was an ambitious venture and, in many respects, a pioneer venture," Schlesinger acknowledged in 1936. "With so much basic research yet to be done, the task was somewhat like trying to write the story of Columbus while he was still sailing westward."[13] The contributing authors' investigations took them to unconventional materials, as their bibliographies testified. They studied structural remains, furniture, and costumes, as well as broadsides, paintings, travel accounts, manuals of etiquette, popular songs, pulp fiction, and other ephemera. Many topics they sought to cover, too, were unorthodox: invention, agriculture, immigration, education, social customs—even society and leisure. If, finally, *The History of American Life* volumes never quite fulfilled their promise in freshness and originality, their contribution to the renewed passion for Americana which flowed through the 1930s like a current should not be underestimated.

3

Not only the motives which drove American writers during the Depression to rediscover their national heritage differed from those of the prewar generation. In its substance too, the past which they recovered was unique. The very character of the primary influence upon the search—the Depression crisis—made it so. Economic dislocation stimulated a renewed interest in history; it also influenced the tone of the revival and the quality of its vision. The effect proved profoundly conservative. Although deeply distressed in their present circumstance, writers who took up historical themes during the 1930s sought neither to lay the blame on their ancestors nor to discredit other eras. They could accuse only themselves of apostasy. Accordingly, they undertook to recover the traditional values and principles which the national experience had validated. Unlike the Young Radicals, the generation which turned to history during the Thirties was preoccupied with the tested and the permanent.

Their very conviction of the utility of the American past represented a significant development. It marked an admission, not always easy for Americans, that their nation could not escape the burdens of history. Moreover, it dictated a specific vision of the past. With the prospect of a placid, harmonious history of no use to them, the writers of the 1930s had perforce to develop a perspective suitable for a time of crisis. The analogies and parallels they sought in the past came from other periods of storm and stress, of chaos and conflict. Accordingly, the norms they found in the story of American development differed little from the conditions of their own time.

In America, as elsewhere, the Depression encouraged an insular nationalism which colored the interpretation of history. But this was neither the chauvinism of the prewar nor the xenophobia of the postwar periods. Americans during the Thirties responded particularly to the native and continental facets of their past; their impulses were isolationist rather than nativist. Thus, the nationalism of the decade stimulated an emphasis upon the uniqueness of American ideas and values, not the purity of any single racial or cultural stock. In many ways, American writers turned their backs on the Old World. Not the seaboard nation of smallclothes, transatlantic citizens, and "Good Feelings" attracted them, but the interior country with its homespun garb, provincial politics, and sectional animosities. The pioneer farmer much more than the merchant trader represented the American character for these twentieth century citizens. They cherished his frontier penchant for tackling problems head-on. And like him, they believed that the solutions lay close at hand. Europe could provide neither guidance nor excuses.

Its democratic tendencies represented still another unique characteristic of the 1930s' search for a usable American past. The leveling influence of the Depression encouraged an emphasis upon the classless, inclusive character of the national experience. In a time of common crisis, the revived past must serve all the people. This led to an accentuation of the most encompassing aspects of the American heritage: the occupations and amusements of the many rather than the manners of the few, the log cabin in the clearing rather than the plantation mansion by the river. The same Americans who acknowledged the "forgotten man"–the farmer and the worker–of their own time also wished to recognize their nameless ancestors who toiled in the fields and factories.

A sense of community, engendered by shared economic adversity, represented another aspect of the egalitarian spirit of the 1930s. Interpreters of the past responded to the mood of national unity, promoted by Franklin D. Roosevelt, which contrasted with the divisive temper of the preceding decade. Rarely speaking now in the solitary accents of a cultural elite, they sought instead to capture a wide and popular hearing. As in other times of crisis, writers turned to the American people for the ultimate verdict upon the national destiny. But the great democratic jury, they believed, must have access to a common historical literature. As a result, in general the gap between the writer and his society narrowed during the Thirties.

For some Americans, of course, the rediscovered past of the 1930s opened up romantic vistas which clashed sharply with the drab Depression foreground. No doubt this helps explain the contemporary vogue of historical novels. Perhaps this trend, best exemplified by the immense popularity of Margaret Mitchell's *Gone with the Wind*, represented very little more than sentimental escapism on the part of millions. But some observers took even this phenomenon as a portent of serious social attitudes. Malcolm Cowley, for example, insisted that "not a few of the historical romancers who flourished in these years revealed a social purpose in their writing: at a time of crisis they were turning toward the past, not simply because it was picturesque but also to find heroes whose example would assure us about the future."[14]

Whatever the implications of developments in historical fiction, a new preoccupation with heroes from the past did indeed constitute one of the key features of the rediscovered American heritage. Appropriately, it found preeminent expression in a sober and solid, a conventional and conservative genre, the venerable life-and-times. The biographical vogue of the Great Depression years was remarkable. No preceding era could compare with it. In 1932, for example, publishers brought out two biographies a day, twice as many as ever before—and the trend continued through the decade. Furthermore, book sales told the same story. The best-seller lists included more and more nonfiction works, with biographies of Americans prominent among them.

For all their interest in life histories, however, Depression readers had little use for the "new biography" of the preceding era. Indeed, as Alfred Kazin put it, "Where the generation of the twenties wanted to revenge themselves on their fathers, the generation of the thirties needed the comfort of their grandfathers." Thus, the army of authors who dusted off the traditional form of biography also approached their subjects with sympathy and respect. The format seldom varied: whether the subject belonged to the first or second rank, he deserved a full account and the reader expected a full accounting in pages cluttered with footnotes and bibliography. The effect was nearly always the same: if the preceding decade had threatened to compromise the reputation of many historic American heroes, the years of the Depression witnessed a great rehabilitation of national statesmen, soldiers, and even scholars. It was a day for the redemption of controversial reputations, and for defending the unjustly maligned. Bernard DeVoto, for example, wrote almost every word of *Mark Twain's America* (1932) to refute the calumnies of Van Wyck Brooks' *The Ordeal of Mark Twain*. But perhaps the latter's *Life of Emerson* (1932) represented the most dramatic example of the new affirmative attitude toward the past. Brooks' subsequent work, particularly the *Makers and Finders* series of literary histories which began to emerge later in the decade, marked an even sharper contrast with that of his prewar years. Now the once-radical author described his purpose as "reviving the special kind of memory that fertilizes the living mind and gives it the sense of a base on which to build."[15]

If Henry Pringle's somewhat hostile biography of *Theodore Roosevelt* (1931) retained traces of a debunking mood completely absent from its successor, the apologetic *Life and Times of William Howard Taft* (2 volumes, 1939), the contrast perhaps revealed something about the impact of the changing times upon an author's view of history. With sympathetic, prize-winning lives of Grover Cleveland and Hamilton Fish, Allan Nevins encouraged readers to reassess the much discredited Gilded Age; and in *John D. Rockefeller* (2 volumes, 1940), the Columbia history professor sought to improve the image of the Robber Barons and their contribution to what he called "the heroic age of American enterprise." Reaching farther back in time, Carl Van Doren paid tribute in 1938 to the first of the enterprising Americans with his best-selling biography of Benjamin Franklin. Besides being a work of scholarship and literary art, *Benjamin Franklin*, a Pulitzer Prize-winner, was a "timely" book. As Carl Becker emphasized in his laudatory review, "no voice from the past speaks with greater pith and relevance to all men of intelligence and good will in the mad world of today. . . ."[16]

Whether recent past or distant, the spirit of the Thirties seemed somehow to improve it. The sturdy full-dress biographies proliferated, one wag observed, even more rapidly than New Deal agencies. Among the many notable new volumes dealing with American lives, a few of the most enduring were: Lloyd Lewis, *Sherman: Fighting Prophet* (1932), which one reviewer hailed appropriately as "old-fashioned"; Claude G. Bowers, *Beveridge and the Progressive Era* (1932); Douglas Southall Freeman's four-volume monument to *R. E. Lee* (1934-35), which Stephen Vincent Benét claimed restored his "faith in biography"; Ralph Barton Perry, *The Thought and Character of William James* (2 volumes, 1935), a Pulitzer Prize-winner like the *Lee*; Philip C. Jessup, *Elihu Root* (2 volumes, 1938); and Henry Seidel Canby, *Thoreau* (1939). All immediately won widespread admiration and respect; many remained unsurpassed for decades afterward.

"Why is it that biographic writing in this country so consistently outruns historical writing?" Allan Nevins wondered aloud in 1939. Perhaps because for many readers and authors, history had become biography. Despite the Marxists and their dialectics about inexorable material forces, many among the generation of the 1930s believed in the power of free men—and wished to read and write about them. Moreover, they found something peculiarly *usable* about biography. Edgar Johnson grasped the idea in 1938, when he wrote: "In recent years a vast exploration has been going on of the heroes of American history and folklore—for what we are is the product of the America that was." More important, he insisted, "the whole American past, mirrored in modern biography, is implicit in contemporary society, infused in contemporary consciousness. Not only is it the soil out of which the present has grown, but our biographers have everywhere been preoccupied with establishing its richness and relevance. . . . And doing so," Johnson concluded, they "have demonstrated that the past is a living part of the present."[17]

4

Every revitalization of the past comes down finally to a concentration upon selected epochs, events and, more important, the personages who figured in them. Not surprisingly, the same characteristics which many Americans chose to emphasize when they recalled their heritage dictated the historical eras they memorialized most frequently and fervently. The emphasis upon the insular and democratic in their experience, the orientation to other eras of crisis, the need for stories which were somehow both romantic and relevant—all these factors led almost inescapably to an absorption in the nineteenth century years of Manifest Destiny and Civil War. In the great "Middle Period" between the Missouri Compromise and Appomattox, more than any other epoch, historical interpreters of the 1930s found the past they sought to revitalize. The issues, developments, and especially the personalities of those years proved compelling to Americans moving toward the middle years of the twentieth century. Personalities because, even in an atmosphere infused with democracy, the people must have their heroes. More than an epoch or an event, a single American could stand for—literally embody—the lessons of the past which the Depression generation sought to recall. But interest and attention centered necessarily upon individuals of a special sort. They must needs be the spokesmen, the representatives, the symbols finally, of the whole people, the common folk. The choices then were obvious. Among literary artists they could only be Twain and Whitman; among Presidents Jackson and preeminently Lincoln.

In Old Hickory and Sam Clemens, in Walt Whitman and most of all in "Honest Abe," the Great Emancipator, the people responded to the highest incarnations of themselves. Here indeed were the great democratic heroes of the nineteenth century past. But what did these four historic personages have in common besides their democratic tendencies? Each of course had emerged, in his own characteristic rough-and-tumble fashion, during the romantic, exuberant antebellum years. Each had about him that homespun coarseness of texture, that pungent tang of the soil which marked him as distinctly, indomitably American. Each had been cut out of the "native grain." From their humble origins all four retained, albeit not without misgivings, warm humanitarian sympathies, a real but studied uncouthness, a tendency to defy polite convention, an earthy sense of humor, a preference for male company, and withal a self-consciousness about their public images. In life, each had stirred the blood of his contemporaries; though long dead now their emotive power remained—altered perhaps, but hardly diminished and probably enhanced. While an Emerson or a Lowell, a Webster or a Clay could inspire respect, his image remained pallid and out of reach. But a Jackson or a Mark Twain immediately conjured up an impression rich in color and application. And Whitman and Lincoln became virtually reincarnated in the minds of millions of Americans.

Appropriately, biographers turned repeatedly to these four personages. The life of Old Hickory was retold in colorful detail with great warmth and vigor in the two celebrated volumes by Marquis James, *Andrew Jackson: The Border Captain* (1933) and *Andrew Jackson: Portrait of a President* (1937), the latter of which won a Pulitzer Prize. Two more sympathetic studies of Samuel Clemens followed DeVoto's during the course of the decade, and Walt Whitman was the subject of four substantial works, including a 1937 biography by Edgar Lee Masters, which one reviewer found "not so soured as . . . his book on Lincoln." That three additional Whitman and two more Mark Twain studies appeared early in the following decade bore further testimony to their hold upon the times.

Above all other historical personages, however, Lincoln came to dominate the era of Franklin D. Roosevelt. In a time of partisan strife and international conflict, the development had profound implications. The Great Emancipator symbolized neither party nor nationality, but freedom and democracy, unity and charity. Moreover, his image revived the memory that, even in a bloody Civil War, the United States had somehow survived. New works dealing with his life both reflected and enhanced his increasing hold upon the imagination of a generation. No wonder Alfred Kazin counted the "passionate addiction to Lincoln" among "the most moving aspects" of the decade.[18]

chapter two

THE EMERGENCE OF THE
LINCOLN IMAGE

1

In the face of many complicated public issues, the dialogue between the leaders and the led in a democracy must perforce find expression in elementary terms. Frequently, simple and unambiguous symbols can stand for the complex clusters of ideals and principles shared by a public consensus. Some symbols, however, provide little more than a generalized emotional response. The flag and the national anthem, for instance, merely reinforce a vague sense of Americanism. But human symbols, heroes from past epochs, often embody specific national values and goals. Accordingly, through them national purposes find articulation in a democracy.

During the crises of the Thirties, many Americans yearned for a human symbol to epitomize the democratic tradition and sustain their commitment to free institutions in the face of adversity. In the past, Thomas Jefferson had served such a purpose. Never neglected long enough to require revival, his image nonetheless underwent inevitable alteration during the Depression. In every preceding era, partisans had invoked Jefferson's name, like that of his arch-rival Alexander Hamilton, to sanction or censure policies and programs at issue. Indeed, the American political dialogue had never digressed far from their terms, whatever the application. But the Twenties belonged to Hamilton. Conservative Republicans on Wall Street and in Washington clamped their chains on him, and Andrew Mellon, touted as "the greatest Secretary of the Treasury since Alexander Hamilton," welded the link between the political and financial capitals with a regressive tax program. When the stock market collapsed, however, the reputation of both Mellon and his reputed mentor plummeted.

Jefferson had not been altogether forgotten during the New Era. Two authors, both with partisan inclinations, sought to confront the Hamiltonian present with a better, Jeffersonian past. Claude G. Bowers, in *Jefferson and Hamilton: The Struggle for Democracy in America* (1925), reached back to the roots of the dialogue, while Vernon Parrington's *Main Currents in American Thought* brought the controversy up to the end of the nineteenth century. While the latter work made its mark mainly in intellectual circles, *Jefferson and Hamilton* won political recognition for both its hero and author.

Franklin D. Roosevelt lauded the Bowers book in a review for the liberal *New York Evening World*. "I felt like saying 'At last' as I read . . . 'Jefferson and Hamilton,' " he declared in commending the "simple historic facts" of the volume to the homes, schools, and, pointedly, editorial rooms of America. More than historical data concerned the aspiring Democratic politician, however. Unlike the newspaper editors who had sneered so recently at his own "mere suggestion that Jeffersonianism could, in any remote manner, bear upon the America of 1925," Roosevelt believed "that the forces hostile to control of government by the people which existed in the crisis of 1790-1800 could still be a threat in our day and land."[1]

In the midst of his own, and the Democratic Party's slow and frustrating convalescence, Roosevelt had already matured the present-minded view of history which he would evince so frequently later in the White House. Accordingly, he prized the Bowers book in particular because it prompted "the constantly recurring thought of parallel or at least analogous situations existing in our own generation." Jeffersonian democracy—and Hamiltonian aristocracy—took on new meaning for the Hyde Park patrician after reading the volume. Then, in Roosevelt's hands, the past became more vital—and *Jefferson and Hamilton* more relevant to contemporary party politics—than even the author had intended. "I have a breathless feeling as I lay down this book," Roosevelt concluded "—a picture of escape after escape which the Nation passed through in those first ten years; a picture of what might have been if the Republic had been finally organized as Alexander Hamilton sought." But, he continued, "I have a breathless feeling, too, as I wonder if, a century and a quarter later, the same contending forces are not again mobilizing."[2]

In reviving the memory of Jefferson, Claude Bowers had obviously also whetted at least one Democrat's appetite for political battle. Thus inspired, the party rewarded the author in 1928 by naming him to keynote their national convention. The Democrats may have recovered their birthright, but as the election returns suggested, they had not yet found a winning candidate. Thus, while the Republicans celebrated their victory, their opponents sought to uncover another Thomas Jefferson. Or, as Roosevelt put it, "Hamiltons we have today. Is a Jefferson on the horizon?"

In Franklin Roosevelt some soon found him, as the candidate had intended during the 1932 presidential campaign. After the inauguration, others felt betrayed. The Jefferson postage stamp and nickel, even the Jefferson Memorial and Roosevelt's Charlottesville speeches, were not enough. What-

ever the ties between Monticello and Hyde Park, many saw
the discredited shadow of Alexander Hamilton lurking behind the New Deal. While Roosevelt spoke in the Jeffersonian
idiom, his advisers planned in Federalist terms. Opponents of
the Administration and its programs found ammunition for
their attacks in the *laissez-faire* and states rights doctrines so
often identified with the Author of the Declaration of Independence. The New Deal gradually forced a reversal of roles,
as the journalist Irving Brant pointed out. "It has turned
Hamiltonian Nationalists into weeping mourners for the lost
sovereignty of the states. It has turned Jeffersonian States
Righters into the most active Federalists the United States
has ever known."[3]

With the approach of the 1936 election, Jefferson's name
became the rallying cry for many who opposed the New
Deal. Even as they found support for their own views in the
Virginian's canon, they adamantly denied any such authority
to the Administration. Not only Republicans but members of
the President's own party denounced the New Deal in such
terms. When Al Smith addressed the anti-Roosevelt Liberty
League at a gala Washington banquet early in 1936, he had
already proclaimed himself a "Jeffersonian Democrat" in the
pages of *The Outlook*. Not surprisingly, then, he disinherited
the New Dealers. "It's all right with me if they want to
disguise themselves as . . . Karl Marx, or Lenin, or any of the
rest of that bunch," exclaimed the Happy Warrior, "but what
I won't stand for is allowing them to march under the banner
of Jefferson, Jackson, or Cleveland!"[4] It made little differ-
ence to its critics that the New Deal had, some observers felt,
recently shifted to a more Brandeisian—hence Jeffersonian—
stance. They maintained their attacks.

At the polls in 1936, Franklin Roosevelt triumphed over
his opponents. But, whatever the justification, Jefferson had
become the symbol of antagonism to the New Deal. His name
had thereby lost its usefulness to the President. Perhaps it

was only another reflection of the character of Jeffersonianism—always more potent in opposition than in command.
Regardless, the President, the people, and the times demanded a new, unifying national image. It had already been
created in other quarters.

2

Before the end of Franklin Roosevelt's second term, the
image of Abraham Lincoln had emerged as the fulfillment of
the search for a usable American past. One of the paradoxes
of American history arises from the contrasting functions of
the Jefferson and Lincoln images. That of the President
whose election inaugurated an era of effective one-party
government later created dissension while that of the leader
whose election sundered the Union became transformed into
a unifying force. Moreover, the man whose name in his own
time was anathema to the South became symbolic of the
American nation while that of the Author of tho Declaration
of Independence came increasingly to be invoked in behalf of
sectionalism. This curious phenomenon was never more conspicuous than during the New Deal years. If, before losing its
usefulness, a renewed Jefferson symbol provided a partisan
standard for the campaign and election of 1932, the emergence of the Lincoln image in Roosevelt's second administration indicated an ambition to weld a unified coalition. For all
its differences from the Jefferson symbol, however, that of
Lincoln also had roots in the Twenties.

In those years, Carl Sandburg and Stephen Vincent Benét
had created a Lincoln image around which Americans could
rally when the time came to revive the national past. Turning
away from the contemporary heroes of the Prosperity
Decade, the two poets had rediscovered the rawboned railsplitter who became the Civil War President. For them, the

Lincoln revival represented a reaffirmation of their faith in the people. Indeed, Carl Sandburg drew inspiration from Walt Whitman, the Poet of Democracy, who had come "swaggering from among the hackmen and Broadway bus drivers, out of street swarms and ferry boat crowds, in shirt-sleeves and knockabout clothes" to feel and proclaim his unity with the populace.[5] Whitman found poetry in the streets of New York; Sandburg in the streets of Chicago—in the "bareheaded, shoveling, wrecking, planning, building, breaking, rebuilding" capital of the Heartland. There he discovered the people—on the Halsted Street Car, in back alleys, on the Clark Street Bridge, on picnic boats—became their bard, and announced, in Whitmanesque verse:

I am the people—the mob—the crowd—the mass.
Do you know that lll the great work of the world is
    done through me?
I am the workingman, the inventor, the maker of the
    world's food and clothes.
I am the audience that witnesses history. The
    Napoleons came from me and the Lincolns. They
    die. And then I send forth more Napoleons
    and Lincolns.[6]

Lincoln. Not since Whitman had a poet found such identification with the Great Emancipator. Stuart Sherman summed up the ties between Sandburg and Lincoln: "They are good companions, the two of them, and mutually illuminating—Illinoisians both, plain people, admirable story tellers, rationalists, Jeffersonian democrats both, both non-professing Christians . . . and both poets withal. . . ."[7] After the Armistice Sandburg had begun the search for Lincoln materials which occupied him for two decades afterward. Though never neglecting written sources, he remained in spirit a poet. If he went to the Loop to hear the idiom of his own day, Sandburg sought the voice of the past on the prairies. There he retraced Lincoln's steps, stopping to converse with everyone who had something to say: above all Sandburg wanted to reveal the Lincoln who dwelt in the hearts of the people who had known him.

Finally, steeped in Lincoln lore, Sandburg began to write. The two solid volumes of *Abraham Lincoln: The Prairie Years* appeared in 1926. Readers quickly recognized that the work bore slight resemblance to other biographies, of either past or present. It shared little with the Victorian tradition: the conception was imaginative, the portrayal colorful, the language colloquial. It shared even less with the "new" biography: the research was thorough, the approach sympathetic, the meaning complex. Sandburg sought neither to debunk the reputation nor dissect the personality. On the other hand, Lincoln required no apologist. America, however, needed a new encounter with the best in its past. As Sandburg explained it in his preface,

> Perhaps poetry, art, human behavior in this country, which has need to build on its own traditions, would be served by a life of Lincoln stressing the fifty-two years previous to his Presidency. Such a book would imply that if he was what he was during those first fifty-two years of his life it was nearly inevitable that he would be what he proved to be in the last four.[8]

The prairie years were the formative years: the secret of Lincoln's character, according to Sandburg, was rooted in the Heartland. Hardly a novel idea, this emphasis upon the Great Emancipator's frontier origins received unparalleled exposition in the poet's affectionate portrait. Sandburg, who loved Lincoln's land, limned the formative environment in all its miscellaneous detail. Everybody and everything that somehow touched the life of his subject Sandburg presented in Whitmanesque catalogues. Out of the crowded, episodic structure emerged a panoramic portrait of the man and his times. In the course of the account, Lincoln spoke through letters and speeches and appeared in the eyes of his contemporaries. The ultimate source of the portrait, however, was Sandburg's intuition. Where the sources failed to enlighten, he illuminated the conception with a poetic imagination tempered by immersion in the literature of this subject.

In the author's view, for example, the interaction of environment and personality created a tension in Lincoln. The
tension molded a complex character. "It was noticed among
men that he had two shifting moods, the one of the rollick-
ing, droll story and the one when he lapsed into a gravity
beyond any bystander to penetrate."[9] Character and destiny
thus combined to produce the man who rose from frontier
obscurity to confront the greatest challenge to the nation.
The Great Emancipator had emerged from the people—the
embodiment of their collective capacities and aspirations. As
a man of the people, Sandburg's Lincoln justified American
democracy. His Lincoln was a folk hero.

3

Though as different from Sandburg in character and experience as Paris from prairie, Stephen Vincent Benét shared the
Chicagoan's profound patriotism, and, like him, caught the
vision of America which Whitman had perceived and Lincoln
sustained. Benét's response took the form of the Civil War
epic Whitman had never written. Indeed, Henry Seidel Canby
hailed him as "the poet so urgently called for by our last
national poet. . . ."[10] No American writer had ever undertaken a more ambitious poetic treatment of a national theme
than Benét in *John Brown's Body*, published in 1928.

Like so many artists of his generation, Benét had com-
posed his work abroad. "If this is what comes of sending
poets to Paris on a Guggenheim Fellowship," Canby exclaimed, "let us send them all there."[11] Benét's residence in
France heightened his sense of nationality. "I shall not rest
quiet at Montparnasse," he wrote. "Bury my heart at
Wounded Knee." Dissatisfied with the American present, he
returned to the national past. His poem boldly defied many

of the cultural trends of the Twenties: in an era of self-conscious cosmopolitanism, it celebrated an unrestrained nationalism; in the face of a revolt against the American past, it recreated the Civil War; in the age of Henry Ford, it revived Lincoln and Lee; against the tide of short, esoteric verse, it launched popular epic lines by the hundreds.

John Brown's Body commenced almost where Sandburg's biography concluded. That was only one of the many connections between the two epics. Benet's poem also relied on the historical sources, as an unorthodox prefatory note testified. It, too, bulged with the life, color, and drama of the time—product of the same rare combination of scholarship and imagination which characterized *The Prairie Years*. Benet's portrait of the Great Emancipator also gave further strength to the image, with its combination of brooding mind and benign spirit, that Sandburg had created. The move to the White House only compounded the influences of the prairies by adding the colossal burden of disunion. Lincoln faced it with mixed doubt and self-confidence.

> And as for me—if anyone else comes by
> Who shows me that he can manage this job of mine
> Better than I can—well, he can have the job.
> . . .
> But I haven't run into that fellow yet
> And until or supposing I meet him, the job's my job
> And nobody ele's.

Gaunt, grim, and alone, he came to embody the democratic purpose: "Only Lincoln, awkwardly enduring, confused by a thousand counsels, is neither overwhelmed nor touched to folly by the madness that runs along the streets like a dog in August. . . ." Lincoln and Union—now elevated to a level larger than life. "His huge, patient, laborious hands start kneading the stuff of the Union together again. . . ." Lincoln had grown:

> A tempering of will in these trotting months
> Whose strong hoofs striking have scarred him again and again.

> He still rules more by the rein than by whip or spur
> But the reins are fast in his hands and the horses know it.
> He no longer says "I think," but "I have decided."

And in his determination Lincoln came to embody the spirit of the nation mobilized to preserve the Union and its meaning.

> We can fail and fail,
> But, deep against the failure, something wars,
> Something goes forward, something lights a match,
> Something gets up from Sangamon County ground
> Armed with a bitten and a blunted axe
> And after twenty thousand wasted strokes
> Brings the tall hemlock crashing to the ground.

With the people, incarnate in Lincoln, rising from the earth to protect it, the Union would be preserved. Of such stuff are myths made.[12]

In a biography which read like an epic poem in prose and in a book-length poem which hewed close to the historical record, a Lincoln portrait took shape during the 1920s. In general, the reviewers extended a warm welcome to the new image and the reading public responded enthusiastically. *John Brown's Body*, an early Book-of-the-Month Club selection, sold over one hundred thousand copies in its first year, while almost fifty thousand sets of Sandburg's work were purchased, at ten dollars apiece, in the year after its publication. Through the creation of a Lincoln image sufficient to embody national democratic aspirations, the two poets had partially recovered the promise of the American tradition even before the Great Crash.

4

The Depression generation could choose from a veritable library of Lincoln literature. Books had begun to appear in the Great Emancipator's ‹ , ∷ time, and myths had taken form following his assassination, as Lloyd Lewis demonstrated in *Myths After Lincoln* (1929), and then ramified in the succeeding decades. Indeed, by 1935, Roy P. Basler felt justified in publishing *The Lincoln Legend: A Study in Changing Conceptions*. Concluding his survey of the Lincoln literature, the author marveled how "this extraordinary human being has captured the imagination of two generations of poets, dramatists, novelists, historians, and biographers." Furthermore, Basler saw "no evidence that interest is flagging."[13]

In sheer quantity alone, the literary output of the following years bore Basler out. More important, the character of some of the new works, drawing from the insights of Sandburg and Benét, revealed the changed temper of the national mood. Even Basler's detailed discussion of the earlier myths both reflected and contributed to the new conception—concluding at one point that it "may well be wondered whether there is ever to be a poet capable of fathoming Lincoln."[14] Probably not. But two poets had created the modern myth, and now a lesser imagination transferred it to the stage.

The New Deal primed the pump which tapped one of the sources of the new Lincoln image. E. P. Conkle's *Prologue to Glory*, produced by the WPA's Federal Theatre in 1938, represented the initial imaginative portrayal of Lincoln in the atmosphere created by the renewed search for the American past. Not the statesman of war councils, spoils seekers, and cabinet intrigues, however. The play revealed instead a 22-year-old rustic son of the Middle Border, unconsciously standing on the threshold of the first innocent decisions which would set him on the road to destiny. Rich in the local color, rough-hewn characters, pungent language, and violent action of the frontier, it reflected Carl Sandburg's emphasis upon the pioneer experience as decisive in making the man who became President.

Prologue to Glory sought its authority in the bosoms of
the common people rather than the dry documents of the
past. As the playwright put it, "This play makes no attempt
to be true in all its historical details, it attempts, rather, to be
true to the spirit of the times and the leading character."[15]He
had produced a folk drama suffused with poetic truth. If
Americans wanted a common man's Lincoln with whom they
could identify, Conkle's conception seemed appropriate. The
historical reference of the audience provided the context of
the character, while the awkard but appealing young man
portrayed in the play won their affection.

In eight lively scenes, "set in and about New Salem,
Illinois, around the year 1831," *Prologue to Glory* promoted
the romantic notion that Lincoln's character and destiny
were determined by the love and loss of the legendary Ann
Rutledge. Conkle's portrait of an unambitious frontiersman
goaded into politics by the woman he loved no doubt
humanized Lincoln. But it also simplified and sentimental-
ized him. The central character in the play bore few
resemblances to the later President. As Brooks Atkinson
insisted, "there was a deeper force stirring within" Lincoln
than the playwright managed to suggest.[16] This represented
only one way the play suffered in comparison with *The
Prairie Years*. Carl Sandburg's folk concept of Lincoln had
created a deepened sense of his intrinsically American
wellsprings. On the stage, however, this pioneer heritage
became merely the excuse for a colorful frontier pageant.

E. P. Conkle's innocent mixture of history and romance
provoked an unexpected political attack. Despite one reviewer's claim that *Prologue to Glory* was "100 percent American
in the best and highest sense," and much to Federal Theatre
Director Hallie Flanagan's astonishment, Republican Representative Parnell Thomas, a member of the Dies Committee
on Un-American Activities, condemned the play as well as
another WPA production for "communistic leanings." In a

syndicated newspaper article, the Congressman carried his crusade to the public. "The play *Prologue to Glory* deals with Lincoln in his youth and portrays him battling with the politicians. This is simply a propaganda play to prove that all politicians are crooked."[17]

Absurd as it was, the Republican Representative's attack reflected the supercharged political atmosphere of 1938. However much he might try to intimidate the Federal Theatre, Thomas could not silence the popular clamor for dramas recreating the American past in human—even contemporary—terms that the project had helped raise. As its indefatigable director reported: "Federal Theatre has from the first liked particularly plays of pioneer America. . . ." Abraham Lincoln was only one of the many "historic or legendary figures seen upon our stages." But none of the other WPA historical dramas matched the success of *Prologue to Glory*. Besides a Broadway run of 169 performances, it played in nineteen other cities.[18]

The Federal Theatre indeed had a hit. Audiences responded to the succession of brief, action-filled scenes, the picturesque pageantry, and the underlying sense of anticipation of greater events ahead—so characteristic of the New Deal era. But no matter how popular and engaging, the Conkle play remained a modest attempt at historical characterization. A much fuller embodiment of the new Lincoln image waited just offstage in the wings.

chapter three

ABE LINCOLN IN ILLINOIS:
PAGEANT AND EXHORTATION

1

Robert E. Sherwood's play, *Abe Lincoln in Illinois*, which opened on Broadway October 15, 1938, marked the culmination of the search for a usable American past first by recreating a living Lincoln who epitomized the national purpose and then by enrolling him under the New Deal banner. At the box office and in the press, the drama evoked a response which only the thorough interaction of an author and his times can explain. Before closing, 472 performances later, *Abe Lincoln in Illinois* had become an American institution. The Pulitzer Prize merely ratified the public verdict. The uncommonly faithful film adaptation, produced in 1940, brought the drama to every neighborhood in the land—as well as to the White House.

Rather than a prophet, Sherwood was, in his biographer John Mason Brown's words, a "mirror to his times." A living Lincoln had no more been a part of his conscious heritage than of the rest of his generation. But reading Carl Sandburg's herald of the resurgent national biography, *The Prairie Years*, gave flesh to the playwright's conception. "Up to then," he admitted, "I'd thought that [Lincoln] was a statue, even while he was living." After the encounter came the continual "feeling of kinship," as his friend and colleague Maxwell Anderson expressed it. Identification comprised a part of it: Sherwood found reflections of his own personality and outlook, not to mention physical stature, in the melancholy Lincoln. Respect for Lincoln's intellect also counted: judging from *Abe Lincoln in Illinois*, it was clear to Brooks Atkinson that Sherwood prized "the sweep and scope of his mind."[1]

"It was Sandburg who guided me back to the main sources of Lincoln lore, made me wish to know more of the forces, from without him and within, which shaped this strange, gentle genius," Sherwood wrote in his notes to the play.[2] Elmer Rice recalled that Sherwood had even chosen "The Prairie Years" as the original title of his play. As if to make the connections manifest, Sandburg contributed a brief preface to the published edition of *Abe Lincoln in Illinois*. In addition, *The Prairie Years* no doubt partially influenced Sherwood's choice of the apprenticeship rather than the triumph or the tragedy. Sandburg had been the first writer to treat fully the early years of Lincoln. And, as one drama critic said, "The foreshadowing of the older Lincoln in the younger with all the natural background that bred him was so splendidly achieved in Carl Sandburg's *Prairie Years* it is meet that this memorial to it has been fashioned by Sherwood in the play that the book inspired."[3]

Preeminently, *Abe Lincoln in Illinois* was a historical drama. It partook of the contemporary preoccupation with the American past, including the fascination with historical fact. Thus, to the published edition of his play, Robert Sherwood appended over fifty pages on "The Substance of 'Abe Lincoln in Illinois.'" There, in a scene-by-scene discussion, he indicated the principal historical sources of his drama and cited the documents from which he had taken

Lincoln's words. Although the "playwright's chief stock in trade is feelings, not facts," he felt that "in the case of a play about the development of the extraordinary character of Abraham Lincoln, a strict regard for the plain truth is more than obligatory; it is obviously desirable." By 1938, Sherwood valued "plain truth" even more than poetic truth. Above all, he wanted his audience to believe—and in an age of hard-bitten realities, he preferred to appeal to the mind than the imagination.[4]

2

In structure, Sherwood's play consisted of twelve loosely knit scenes extending over thirty years of Lincoln's life on the prairies. What the playwright sought to create was a drama of preparation and growth, "a play about the solidification of Lincoln himself—a long, uncertain process, effected by influences some of which came from within his own reasoning mind, some from his surrounding circumstances, some from sources which we cannot comprehend." Emphasis fell upon separate stages of Lincoln's growth, captured in individual scenes, rather than upon continuity of characters and action. Sherwood acknowledged that he depended upon the audience's familiarity with his subject to compensate for the episodic structure of the play. He had sought to dramatize "as many as possible" of the influences upon Lincoln. But many other factors had to be "left to the imagination of the audience, because they are beyond mine."[5]

No matter how diffuse it appeared, *Abe Lincoln in Illinois* contained a unity which its very division into three acts revealed. In common with Conkle's play, the three disparate scenes of Act One were laid "in and about New Salem, Illinois in the 1830's." More important, each contributed insights into the formative influences upon the young Lincoln's character. Of these, judging from Sherwood's play, the chief was the love and loss of the same Ann Rutledge who had dominated *Prologue to Glory*. In this romanticized version, she inspired the compassionate faith in humanity which later sustained the older Lincoln of the Civil War years.

If the molding of Lincoln's character constituted the dominant concern of the first act, the compelling question of his destiny commanded the five scenes of the second act. This time the city and environs of Springfield, Illinois in the late 1840s provided a common locale. Again a woman, the very palpable Mary Todd, served as Sherwood's *deus ex machina* in these related scenes. Through the agency of Ann Rutledge Abe Lincoln had deepened his character; in Mary Todd he reluctantly accepted his destiny. This selfish woman personified the duty which Sherwood's protagonist must ultimately embrace. In the scenes of the second act, the playwright charted Lincoln's vacillating voyage toward the resolution that clinched his career. Then, with Lincoln prepared to fulfill his "magnificent destiny," the third act could transform the play from a drama of personal resolution into a pageant of political life in the critical decade leading up to the secession crisis foreshadowed throughout.

As Elmer Rice recalled it, through the first two acts of *Abe Lincoln in Illinois*, he and Robert Sherwood watched with mounting anxiety as the opening night audience remained unmoved by the play. "However," Rice wrote in his autobiography, "the opening scene of the third act . . . evoked a great round of applause; from there on the intensity of response increased."[6] In the third act, Sherwood fore-shortened time and increased tempo. The four scenes centered in Springfield during the pivotal years from 1858 to 1861. They included the Lincoln-Douglas debate which roused the first-nighters, Lincoln's interview with the Repub-

lican kingmakers, election night at his campaign head-
quarters, and the President-elect's departure for Washington
from the railroad depot. Here was a Lincoln the audience
knew, words and deeds they recognized. Sherwood had
intended to capture them with a humanized portrait of the
young Lincoln. Instead, he succeeded by permitting them to
witness recreated the mature Lincoln in historical scenes of
which they had long heard. Raymond Massey, authentic
enough as the youthful railsplitter, became in the third act a
virtual incarnation of the aspiring middle-aged politician.
Moreover, the speeches he delivered now had been con-
structed by Sherwood out of Lincoln's own utterances. This
was living history indeed.

3

The author of *Abe Lincoln in Illinois* put great stock in the
contemporary relevance of his play. "I hope that some day
you will honor this play with your presence," he wrote
President Roosevelt. "I think it shows quite clearly how
Lincoln stood on most present issues in our own country and
abroad."[7] With consummate craftsmanship Sherwood had set
up his third act for such purposes. In staging a recreation of
one of the historic debates with Douglas, Sherwood chose a
format of irresistible drama and undeniable authority. In
utilizing the familiar phrases of the man who became the
Great Emancipator, he compounded the effect of authenticity.

For all his historical validity, Sherwood's Lincoln also
served a partisan purpose. Perhaps, at the time, as Harold
Clurman recalled twenty-five years later, "the country was of
an emphatically liberal disposition." Regardless, it responded
sympathetically and enthusiastically to a play which portrayed a liberal Lincoln. Though the words were Lincoln's,

Franklin Roosevelt could hardly have improved upon them. As one writer put it, "Probably no one in contemporary life could speak with so much authority on this problem of today as Lincoln spoke in the words of yesterday. . . ." The man who delivered Lincoln's speeches onstage, Raymond Massey, specifically linked the two chief executives. "The Civil War President, he believes, was definitely a New Dealer, broadly speaking . . . ," *The New York Times* reported. "Roosevelt, party issues aside, stands in the broad tradition for which Lincoln fought, according to Mr. Massey."[8]

To get across much of his message, Sherwood chose the most primitive of dramatic methods: a ten-minute speech delivered by Lincoln directly to the audience. But in the context of the Lincoln-Douglas debates, it proved both popular and effective. In reprinting it, *The New York Times* called Lincoln's rebuttal of Douglas the "most renowned speech" in the play, and "one applicable to current events as well as to events preceding the Civil War."[9]

Among the pertinent topics with which the speech deals, labor, the Supreme Court, and racial discrimination stand out. In the wake of the violent automobile and steel strikes of 1937, Broadway audiences must have been startled to hear Lincoln declare, "as an American, I can say—thank God we live under a system by which men have the *right* to strike!" When examined further on the subject by conservative Republican leaders in the next scene, Sherwood's potential candidate is even more outspoken.

> It seems obvious to me that this nation was founded on the supposition that men have the right to protest, violently if need be, against authority that is unjust or oppressive. The Boston Tea Party was a kind of strike. So was the Revolution itself.[10]

On the subject of the Supreme Court, only a year after Roosevelt's controversial attempt to "reform" it, Lincoln expresses sentiments which, in Sherwood's opinion, "would constitute political suicide for any candidate for national office today. . . ."

> I am not preaching disrespect for the Supreme Court. I am
> only saying that the decisions of mortal men are often influenced
> by unjudicial bias—and the Supreme Court is composed of mortal
> men, most of whom, it so happens, come from the privileged class
> in the South. There is an old saying that judges are just as honest
> as other men, and not more so; and in case some of you are
> wondering who said that, it was Thomas Jefferson.[11]

Even Lincoln's attack upon slavery, drawn from his extensive
utterances on the subject, had a contemporary ring. Sherwood chose a passage which attacked human bondage in
terms appropriate to his own times.

> It is the old issue of property rights versus human rights—an
> issue that will continue in this country when these poor tongues
> of Judge Douglas and myself shall long have been silent. It is the
> eternal struggle between two principles. The one is the common
> right of humanity, and the other the divine right of kings. It is the
> same spirit that says, "You toil and work and earn bread, and I'll
> eat it." Whether those words come from the mouth of a
> king . . . or from one race of men who seek to enslave another
> race, it is the same tyrannical principle.[12]

No doubt Sherwood, with his uncanny sense of the public
temper, could enlist most of his audience in support of the
sentiments his Lincoln expressed. Anyone who doubted the
historical figure's authorship of the controversial passages,
however, could consult the notes which Sherwood appended
to the published play, as he informed President Roosevelt,
"to assure the reader that I have not distorted Lincoln's
opinions to make them sound applicable to present problems. . . . You, sir," he added parenthetically, "know better
than anyone else just how 'timely' those opinions are." Most
of Sherwood's audience needed no such proof. As *The
Saturday Review of Literature* summed it up early in 1939,
"Lincoln convinced the American people then—and he
convinces us now; Mr. Sherwood's version . . . is so genuine
and real that the reader forgets time and place and is ready to
applaud the sentiment and conclusion which the author puts

into Lincoln's mouth in this, of all years, which is troubled with so many similar problems."[13]

While *Abe Lincoln in Illinois* commented, in verbal terms, upon contemporary domestic issues, it dealt with the international problem on two levels, not the lesser of which was the allegorical. "The development of Lincoln's attitude in the years before the Civil War," the playwright later observed, "paralleled the development of the attitude of the whole American people in the years before 1940."[14] Sherwood doubtless intended to include himself in that generalization. His views had changed markedly in the brief years since 1936, when he wrote his antiwar play, *Idiot's Delight*. The nation now faced the same problems of appeasement and war which had confronted Lincoln. In his allegory Sherwood intended to clarify his own position on the question. Lincoln's transformation from indifference to commitment, which had influenced Sherwood, now provided a lesson which the playwright sought continually to emphasize to his audience. And as the international situation deteriorated still further in the months following the opening of *Abe Lincoln in Illinois*, the parallels between past and present became all the more manifest.

Specific Lincoln speeches in the drama reinforced the lesson of the allegory. Raymond Massey, who delivered them, also commented on the parallels "between Lincoln's fight and ours. . . ." If you "substitute the word dictatorship for the word slavery throughout Sherwood's script," the leading man observed, "it becomes electric with meaning for our time." More than anyone else, the playwright appreciated that fact. When the Munich crisis developed during the rehearsals, Sherwood sought to strengthen the links between the script and the present. "I showed Raymond Massey a passage from Lincoln's Peoria speech, of 1854, which seemed to have a direct bearing on the current situation," he later recalled. "We decided to incorporate this into the speech which Mr. Massey delivered so brilliantly in the debate scene."[15]

The lines had especial pertinence when applied to the current "liberal democratic" point of view—as Sherwood called it—which counseled a "live and let live" attitude toward the dictatorships of Europe. It was an opinion the playwright had once held, just as his Lincoln had once believed that "if the Southern states wanted slavery, they were perfectly free to have slavery." But, by 1938, Sherwood had changed, just as, by 1858, Lincoln had "turned from an appeaser into a fighter." His words, as "blended" by Sherwood in the notable debate scene, carried an unmistakable message to the audience:

> All I am trying to do—now, and as long as I live—is to state and restate the fundamental virtues of our democracy, which have made us great, and which can make us greater. I believe most seriously that the perpetuation of those virtues is now endangered, not only by the honest proponents of slavery, but even more by those who echo Judge Douglas in shouting, "Leave it alone!" This is the complacent policy of indifference to evil, and that policy I cannot but hate. I hate it because of the monstrous injustice of slavery itself. I hate it because it deprives our republic of its just influence in the world; enables the enemies of free institutions everywhere to taunt us as hypocrites; causes the real friends of freedom to doubt our sincerity; and especially because it forces so many good men among ourselves into an open war with the very fundamentals of civil liberty, denying the good faith of the Declaration of Independence, and insisting that there is no right principle of action but *self-interest*. . . .[16]

In the final scene, Sherwood utilized the same effective device he had introduced into the earlier debate scene—a set speech delivered by Lincoln directly to the audience. No doubt the spectacle of the President-elect departing from Springfield to lead a nation on the threshold of war also evoked a sympathetic response because of the conspicuous parallels with the present.

We gained democracy, and now there is the question whether it is fit to survive. Perhaps we have come to the dreadful day of awakening, and the dream is ended. If so, I am afraid it must be ended forever. I cannot believe that ever again will men have the opportunity we have had. Perhaps we should admit that, and concede that our ideals of liberty and equality are decadent and doomed.

"And yet—" neither Lincoln nor Sherwood could end on such a note—"let us believe that it is not true!"[17]

The note of uncertainty on which the play ended was appropriate to the times in which it was produced. "Against the background of American hopes and traditions and determinations," wrote one contemporary, Sherwood's protagonist "points toward democracy's uncertain future, of which the contemporary audience is more aware than any audience to whom Lincoln might have spoken in his own day." Lincoln's farewell speech to the Springfield townspeople thus became the final device for linking the threat of war in 1861 with the predicament of the present.

4

The RKO film production of *Abe Lincoln in Illinois* had its premiere in Washington, D.C., early in 1940. The setting said something about the established place already won by the Sherwood vehicle, which the presence of government and diplomatic dignitaries only confirmed. The First Lady led the guests, who included the secretaries of State, Treasury, Agriculture, and Navy, as well as the British and Italian ambassadors.

The movie they saw revealed a rare creative continuity with the play that had tried out before some of the same audience fifteen months earlier. The scenario bore the playwright's stamp: after selling the film rights, Sherwood had rewritten the play for the screen. The actor in the title role, too, was familiar: Raymond Massey recreated his Broadway triumph before the cameras. The episodic or even cinematic character of the play lent itself readily to the motion picture medium. In this screen adaptation the Lincoln story had apparently found its consummate expression. Sherwood, no novice at film-making and therefore aware of its unique possibilities, nevertheless stayed close to his playscript. "The picture is faithful to the play," he wrote afterward. And one reviewer pronounced *Abe Lincoln in Illinois* "probably as successful a transference to the films of a serious and ambitious stage production as has ever been managed. . . ."[18]

The film was also faithful to the past. While on location for the picture, Raymond Massey had assured a *New York Times* reporter that the scenario "takes virtually no liberties with history." The preoccupation with historical accuracy reflected the mood of the day—far from the irreverence of the Twenties. Massey's portrayal of Lincoln, "a dramatic classic now," came in for its full share of praise. Characteristically, the highest form of tribute emphasized the authenticity of his interpretation. In one reviewer's judgment, Massey succeeded "in portraying Lincoln as a real and complicated man. . . ." The criterion of historical reliability also controlled critical responses to the content of the film. Reviewers reserved their highest accolades for the Lincoln-Douglas debate episode, adapted from the scene which had captured theatre audiences. *Life* magazine proclaimed Massey's delivery of the six-minute Lincoln rebuttal "one of the most thrilling sequences ever filmed." Although reduced considerably for the film version, the speech nevertheless proved timely enough to prompt a brief exchange at a presidential press conference. Franklin Roosevelt had invited Sherwood and Massey to a special showing of the movie at the White House, the night before it premiered downtown. Now a reporter wanted to know how the President had liked

"the way they scrambled up the Lincoln-Douglas debate."
But Roosevelt responded by referring cryptically to something much more ominous: "the way Pennsylvania tried to
cut it down through censorship."[19] However authentic, it
seemed, Sherwood's liberal Lincoln was not above political
controversy.

5

By 1940, *Abe Lincoln in Illinois*—whether on stage or
film—had become a staple of contemporary American culture. But Sherwood's creation represented perhaps only the
most notable manifestation of the contemporary outpouring
of Lincolniana. Surveying this phenomenon from his vantage
point in the commodious "Easy Chair" of *Harper's Magazine*,
Bernard DeVoto interpreted its significance with characteristic conviction. "There is only one explanation for this
intensified interest in a President who has been dead for
three-quarters of a century: it is an invocation," he declared.
"At a time when American democracy has reached a crisis
which many think it cannot survive, the American people
have invoked the man who, by general consent, represents
the highest reach of the American character and who, in an
earlier crisis, best embodied the strength of our
democracy."[20]

The emergence of Lincoln as the apotheosis of the usable
American past, while perhaps not quite the sweeping cultural
development DeVoto described, was nevertheless significant.
It virtually dictated the shape of subsequent renderings of the
Great Emancipator. Whether presented as fact or fiction, the
Lincoln story must contain the requisite amounts of edifica-
tion and inspiration. New versions would necessarily be
evaluated according to that standard. Thus, the publication in
1939 of Carl Sandburg's new Lincoln biography offered a

case study of the process. The reviewers' reception of *The War Years* told almost as much about the new Lincoln image as the book itself.

chapter four

THE LINCOLN OF SANDBURG
AND HIS ADMIRERS

1

"In 1928 I made my decision," Carl Sandburg recalled decades afterward. "I would take my chances on doing the war years." Eleven years later the four stately volumes of *Abraham Lincoln: The War Years* appeared. Completed, the Lincoln project—outstripping in size the Bible, Shakespeare, and every other biography of the Great Emancipator— dwarfed its initial conception. *The Prairie Years* had grown out of a projected children's book; its sequel had been transmuted from a sixteen-page preface. "This introduction," as the author had originally conceived it, "would begin at the death of Lincoln and work back to the day he left Illinois." "There was valor in my innocence!" he later ruefully admitted. Not content with the brief treatment, however, Sandburg undertook an extended version which eventually spilled across 3,400 manuscript pages.[1]

Whatever inspired the poet to embark on an enterprise which often demanded prolonged days in his study, he never sought insulation from the cold winds of the Depression that rattled his attic workshop. In the face of national adversity,

Sandburg drew strength from the source of Lincoln's endurance—humanity. The yield was his poetic testament to the common man, *The People, Yes*, published in 1936, "my footnote to the last words of the Gettysburg Address." Whatever sustained Sandburg in his monumental literary tasks also provided him with resources to embolden the people in their despair. Perhaps he had found inspiration in the author of the New Deal. As the scholar Richard Crowder has observed, the poem which Sandburg "gave to his country when the Great Depression had drained the country of hope, of enterprise, of energy, had about it an aura of Rooseveltian optimism, however vaguely defined the goals."[2]

Nowhere did that hope find more appropriate expression than in the lines in which the poet wove Lincoln's words with his own.

> Lincoln?
> He was a mystery in smoke and flags
> saying yes to the smoke, yes to the flags,
> yes to the paradoxes of democracy,
> yes to the hopes of government
> of the people by the people for the people,
> no to debauchery of the public mind,
> no to personal malice nursed and fed,
> yes to the Constitution when a help,
> no to the Constitution when a hindrance,
> yes to man as a struggler amid illusions,
> each man fated to answer for himself:
> Which of the faiths and illusions of mankind
> must I choose for my own sustaining light
> to bring me beyond the present wilderness?[3]

After what he called his "detour" into the long free verse poem, Sandburg returned to his Lincoln biography, the pause having provided time "to feel the scale and proportion better for the final quarter." The publication of *Abraham Lincoln: The War Years*, at the end of 1939, was a public event. A distinguished group of writers reviewed the book prominently and at great length in leading journals and newspapers. Sandburg's publishers even reprinted a handful of the critical essays, distinguished by "the authority of their judgments and the grace of their style," in pamphlet form.[4] From the beginning, the response of eminent readers was accorded almost the same respect as the work: book reviews too became part of the Lincoln literature.

2

A work of such dimensions as *The War Years* provoked a variety of reactions from the reviewers. Its sheer size left the historian James G. Randall almost speechless. "What we have before us," he gasped, "is the world's longest life of Lincoln." Stephen Vincent Benét called it "a mountain range of a book." The week's reading it required had nearly finished the "dim eyes" of Charles Beard. Still, the renowned historian could perceive that nothing like it had ever before "appeared on land or sea." Each reviewer found a particular theme which he emphasized. According to Lloyd Lewis, "Sandburg the writer, while giving the most catholic of evaluations to date, would seem, by his emphasis, to feel that it was as a user of words that Lincoln shone the brightest." Impressed by another, larger aspect of *The War Years*, Allan Nevins pronounced it "perhaps the best picture of a nation in racked travail yet written by any pen." Henry Bertram Hill of the *Kansas City Star* pointed out the prominent position occupied by the common people, concluding that "these volumes in reality constitute an apotheosis of the American people as well as of Lincoln as the great exemplar of their essential worth and goodness."[5]

All agreed, however, on certain judgments. For one, as Lloyd Lewis put it, "Sandburg was born to this particular job. . . ." "The poets have always understood Lincoln, from Whitman and Emerson to Lindsay and Benét," wrote another historian, Henry Steele Commager, "and it is fitting that from the pen of a poet should come the greatest of all Lincoln biographies. . . ." As the youthful liberal journalist Max Lerner confessed, "I generally distrust the meeting of perfect writer and perfect theme." But, the "surprising thing about Sandburg writing on Lincoln is that the results are good. . . ." The author's exhaustive research and breadth of viewpoint impressed Allan Nevins. "He commands five rays of light on the man and his times to every one that a writer of a generation ago would have possessed." Finally, James G. Randall summed up Sandburg's peculiar qualifications for the task: "a rare feeling for Lincoln, a life absorption in the subject, a burning desire to produce the saga, a marathon-like endurance over decades of prodigious labor, a poet's sense of language, a flair for pithy phrasing, a robust personality spiced with the tang of the prairies, and an ability to combine realistic detail with emotional appreciation."[6]

Recalling the imaginative flights of Sandburg's two volumes on the prairie years, the reviewers applauded the more subdued strain of the new work. Faced with "fewer documents and many more myths" when he set out to write about Lincoln's early years, as Robert Sherwood explained it, the poet "gave greater play to his own lyrical imagination." In *The War Years*, however, "he sticks to the documentary evidence, gathering from a fabulous number of sources."[7] None of the critics, however, caught the uniquely appropriate character of the contrast between the two Lincoln books. Just as Sandburg's poetic treatment of the prairie years suited, in subject as well as mood, the spirit of the Twenties, his somber, documented narrative of the war years, with its tragic conclusion, fit the temper of the late Thirties.

The documentary character of *The War Years* derived from extensive quotation of the sources. Such a technique allowed little opportunity for interpretation, a fact which a number of reviewers acknowledged. "It is all narrative," wrote Henry Steele Commager, "the analysis takes care of itself, and the

interpretation is implicit in the material and the presentation." Sandburg's arrangement of his material, according to
Charles Beard, resembled more "a diary or saga than a
systematic presentation." While the author attempted no
explicit analysis, a definite interpretation of Lincoln emerged
from his biography nonetheless, as Allan Nevins pointed out.
"In essentials it is the familiar portrait. . . . we see again the
Lincoln of Lowell, of Carl Schurz, and of Lord Charnwood;
for the world has never been in doubt as to its principal
attributes."[8]

3

Though Sandburg's closely documented narrative method
afforded little opportunity for interpretation, on occasion he
intruded his personality upon the work, not merely in his
manipulation of contemporary evaluations of Lincoln, but in
his own implicit judgments. At every turn, the long, winding
biography bore the marks of the author's hand and intelligence. The portrait was cumulative, gaining shape and
substance as Lincoln took hold of himself and the national
crisis. After his first forceful steps to provision Fort Sumter,
Sandburg's Lincoln lapsed into an uncertain cadence—interrupted by the recurring threats to resign. His temporizing,
however, reflected the burden of his responsibility, not a
weakness of his will. Sandburg knew this, and attempted to
capture the agony of highest office in a handful of
impressionistic sentences.

> To think incessantly of blood and steel, steel and blood, the
> argument without end by the mouths of brass cannon, of a
> mystic cause carried aloft and sung on dripping and crimson
> bayonet points—to think so and thus across nights and months
> folding up into years, was a wearing and a grinding that brought
> questions. What is this teaching and who learns from it and where
> does it lead? "If we could first know where we are and whither

we are tending, we could better judge what to do and how to do it."

Beyond the black smoke lay what salvations and jubilees? Death was in the air. So was birth. What was dying no man was knowing. What was being born no man could say.[9]

Whatever the cost, the war must be pursued. And as Lincoln rose steadily to the responsibility, he drew strength from the people who had forced it upon him. At the same time, in their consciousness, he became an extension of their own character and purposes.

> At home and abroad judgments came oftener that America had at last a President who was All-American. He embodied his country in that he had no precedents to guide his footsteps; he was not one more individual of a continuing tradition, with the dominant lines of the mold already cast for him by Chief Magistrates who had gone before.
>
> . . .
>
> Also around Lincoln gathered some of the hope that a democracy can choose a man, set him up high with power and honor, and the very act does something to the man himself, raises up new gifts, modulations, controls, outlooks, wisdoms, inside the man, so that he is something else again than he was before they sifted him out and anointed him to take an oath and solemnly sign himself for the hard and terrible, eye-filling and center-staged, role of Head of the Nation.[10]

Before the end of his first administration, Lincoln had become the focus of every eye. The intercourse of his personality and the critical events of the war had made him the embodiment of national purposes—and more. "The man Lincoln, his person and mind, had come to be the pivotal issue of the 1864 campaign," Sandburg observed.

> Some would vote for him with no particular faith, rating him low as statesman and leader, nevertheless preferring him to the only other candidate. Others would vote for him in a loyalty that had seldom or never swerved since he became President; they had arrived at an abiding faith in him. A character and personality had become a reality inwoven with their own hearts and passions. In the chaos of the times he was to these folk a beacon light that shone, that wavered, that in moments almost flickered out into a black despair, yet returned to shine without wavering.[11]

After following Lincoln's lonely journey through the dark months preceding the pivotal election, Sandburg brought him out with the popular vindication, a sobered, even more "unfathomable" man. From then on, pointing toward the eventual victory for the Union and the ultimate martyrdom of its savior, the author emphasized the deeper shades of the man and the rising reverence for him.

> Had the people and events of those tornado years shaped Lincoln more and more into a man paradoxically harder than ever, yet almost more delicate and tenuous in human judgments and affairs? Was there more often a phantom touch in what he did? Did certain men and women who had studied him either close up or from far away feel that a strange shade and a ghost, having often a healing power, moving toward wider and surer human solidarity, lived and spoke in the White House? For such . . . who knew an intimacy with Lincoln even when he was at his loneliest . . . were ready to uphold him when they had no inkling of where his next decision might bring the country. . . .[12]

Sandburg intruded upon the work in another way: in his selection of contemporary interpretations. The poet with his appreciation of Lincoln's character turned to other poets with theirs. Emerson, Thoreau, Hawthorne, Melville, Bryant, Lowell, Whittier—each responded in his own way. Above all, Sandburg encroached upon *The War Years* in the person of his spiritual companion, "the loafer, the lazy, dreaming Walt Whitman . . . prophet of the Average Man, crier of America as the greatest country in the world—in the making."[13] Not altogether unconsciously, Sandburg had sought to make himself the Whitman of his time. To many, he had already fulfilled his predecessor's prescription for the poet, "that his country absorbs him as affectionately as he has absorbed it."

From free verse in the Whitman manner, Sandburg had now turned to a prose epic of the national crisis in which the Solitary Singer had figured, albeit inconspicuously. In *The War Years* Whitman became a seemingly ubiquitous presence, sauntering over the capital, haunting the hospitals, remarking the movement of troops, but most of all, scrutinizing the

President. "Quaker-blooded, softhearted, sentimental, a little crazy," he brought deep understanding in the face of shallow prejudice. "I believe fully in Lincoln," Whitman wrote, "—few know the rocks and quicksands he has to steer through." Unlike the favor-seeking opportunists who badgered the President, the gentle, charitable poet never sought access to the man he reverenced above all others. Whitman remained content to hover always in the shadowy wings— "one of the background spokesmen of democracy in the Lincoln scene"—expressing an almost maternal concern for the President to his diary and correspondents.[14]

Like many others, Whitman gazed intently upon the Great Emancipator's care-worn face. He saw "a deep latent sadness in the expression" which none of the artists had captured. In Sandburg's reading, the poet became the eyes—the soul—of the People, somehow in their greater silence sustaining the lonely man in the White House. "Whitman with the passing months felt a deepening faith in the gifts and the face of Lincoln." "I think well of the President," the poet wrote, "he has shown I sometimes think an almost supernatural tact in keeping the ship afloat at all. . . . I say never yet Captain, never ruler, had such a perplexing dangerous task as his the past two years." As Sandburg summed up, "For Whitman, Lincoln was a great voice and a sublime doer in the field of democracy. He regarded both Lincoln and himself as foretellers of a New Time for the common man and woman."[15]

Through more than three bulky volumes, Sandburg moved slowly—almost reluctantly—to the moment of tragedy. Finally, after Lincoln's ominous dream came the fateful Good Friday: "Blood on the Moon." After the assassination, Sandburg summoned up his benediction. "To a deep river, to a far country, to a by-and-by whence no man returns, had gone the child of Nancy Hanks and Tom Lincoln, the wilderness boy who found far lights and tall rainbows to live by, whose name even before he died had become a legend inwoven with men's struggle for freedom the world over."[16]

From every corner of that same earth, Sandburg reported, came the great outpouring of sentiment for the fallen giant in the New World. "A Tree Is Best Measured When It's Down," the poet entitled his chapter of tributes. Near the end, he recorded the reactions of the two men who perhaps meant most to him. Count Leo Tolstoy expressed the best sentiments of the Old World. Traveling in the Caucasus, he found himself confronted by uncivilized tribesmen demanding to know about the "greatest general and greatest ruler of the world." As Sandburg told it, "To Tolstoy the incident proved that in far places over the earth the name of Lincoln was worshiped and the personality of Lincoln had become a world folk legend."[17]

"No music more strange and mystical than that of the poet Walt Whitman," wrote Sandburg as he turned finally to the one person who fully understood Lincoln and completely embraced his vision. No heart more tender and loving, no voice more sincere as he mourned "the sweetest, wisest soul of all my days and lands. . . ." The man who felt the loss perhaps deepest of all never descended to bitterness or vengeance. Father Abraham's magnanimity lived on in Whitman's breast, as Sandburg made clear in a closing paragraph.

> One of his verses saluted "Reconciliation" as the "word over all, beautiful as the sky." Of the four bloody years his line ran: "Beautiful that war and all its deeds of carnage must in time be utterly lost." He had written, for whatever it might mean to anyone: "My enemy is dead, a man as divine as myself is dead." And he compressed both melancholy and solace in his line "The hands of the sisters Death and Night incessantly softly wash again, and ever again, this soil'd world."[18]

4

The torrent of tributes to Lincoln at the end raised *The War Years* to epic proportions only because of the scope and details of the earlier volumes. The varied cries of grief became a national chorus only because the voices of the people had been heard throughout. From the beginning, Sandburg's Lincoln had been surrounded by a moving panorama of people; thus his biography had become a mountain of contemporary testimony. From it emerged an image of Lincoln as a mirror of mankind. No one understood this better than Robert Sherwood, whose Lincoln drama had contained elements of the same image. "Quite properly, Mr. Sandburg's great work is not the story of the one man's life," the playwright observed in his review of *The War Years*. "It is a folk biography. The hopes and apprehensions of millions, their loves and hates, their exultation and despair, were reflected truthfully in the deep waters of Lincoln's being, and so they are reflected truthfully in these volumes."[19]

The man and the people had become inseparable. In 1864, Lincoln had returned to them for their verdict. Sandburg the poet dramatized their response. "The American electorate . . . spoke on whether a colossal, heavy, weary war should go on under the same leadership as it had begun, on whether the same guiding mind and personality should keep the central control and power. To this the electorate, 'We, the people,' by a majority said Yes." The people's mandate brought Lincoln new stature; but he never forgot the source of his strength.

> Out of the smoke and stench, out of the music and violent dreams of the war, Lincoln stood perhaps taller than any other of the many great heroes. This was in the mind of many. None threw a longer shadow than he. And to him the great hero was The People. He could not say too often that he was merely their instrument.[20]

In the trials and triumph of the Union, Lincoln and democracy had become one. That lesson, old as the Lincoln story, gained renewed meaning with Sandburg's telling and new pertinence with the reviewers' interpretations. Even if, as Max Lerner acknowledged, Sandburg had "taken care not to write the sort of contemporary book that underlines the parallels between yesterday and today," some of the critics hastened to read their own lessons. In *The War Years*, Henry Steele Commager and Allan Nevins found implications enough to last for years. According to the former, Sandburg had provided "a portrait from which a whole generation may draw understanding of the past and inspiration for the future." In Nevins' judgment, it was "a narrative which for decades will hearten all believers in the stability of democracy and the potentialities of democratic leadership." Even Max Lerner declared that "It is a bit of luck for us that these volumes should appear just when the question of the conduct of the war by democracies is so much in our minds." Grateful to find "a store of stuff" on the issue in Sandburg's biography, he concluded that "there never was a time when it was more important for us than now to know the capacity of a democracy to turn up greatness of Lincoln's sort from its humblest sons—a greatness that will survive the grime and savagery of war."[21]

Perhaps as much as anyone, Stephen Vincent Benét had contributed to the Lincoln revival and the national reaffirmation. Now he responded characteristically to the contemporary meaning of *The War Years*. Finding in Sandburg's volumes "a renewed faith in the democracy that Lincoln believed in and a renewed belief in the America he sought," Benét commended them to his readers. "They are a good purge for our own troubled time and for its more wild-eyed fears. For here we see the thing working, clumsily, erratically, often unfairly, attacked and reviled by extremists of left and right, yet working and surviving nevertheless." To the author of *John Brown's Body*, the lesson of Carl Sandburg's biography was clear. "And," he concluded, "there never was a better time for it than this year of our Lord 1939."[22] Two years later, even the author acknowledged the contemporary relevance of his volumes when he revised and condensed them to form "A Profile of the Civil War," which he entitled *Storm Over the Land*. "Perhaps the volume can be of use in a time of storm to those inexorably aware 'time is short,' " Sandburg wrote in the preface. "Perhaps they may find shapes of great companions out of the past and possibly touches of instruction not to be used like broken eggs beyond mending."[23]

By the end of the Depression decade, many literate Americans had repossessed a usable past. For them the moral of American history was unmistakable: democracy would persevere even in times of crisis. But that renewed faith did not diminish their need for Sandburg's Lincoln, judging from the enthusiastic response to its publication. His biography provided an inexhaustible treasure of reassuring evidence that the nation could provide both the leadership and the resources to meet even the greatest challenge. Something more, however, lay beneath the lesson of *The War Years*. In the profoundest sense, the usable American past always meant a reaffirmation of faith in the sovereign people—presented to the people from whom, ultimately, the Lincolns and everything else came. In honoring Sandburg's Lincoln, then, readers paid homage to themselves. Lloyd Lewis summed it all up: "The people knew all along—the people, yes!"

chapter five

ROOSEVELT:
THE DEMOCRATIC LINCOLN

1

The study of myths and symbols as keys to the collective mind of a generation or nation emerged with the rise of the Lincoln image. A contemporary student of American thought and a pioneer in the use of the new intellectual tools, Ralph Henry Gabriel fostered one development while he acknowledged the other. His major contribution was an influential interpretation, *The Course of American Democratic Thought*, published in 1940, itself part of the renewed search for a usable national past. "After Appomattox and particularly after 1900," the author wrote in a chapter on "The New American Symbolism," "the place once held in American democratic symbolism by the Declaration was taken by the Constitution, and the figure of Washington was replaced by that of Lincoln." Gabriel conceded that the "austere first President remains today an important national symbol, but he is no longer first in the hearts of his countrymen. Lincoln holds that place. . . ." Everywhere the author found evidence for his assertion. "It consists primarily in the use of Lincoln's words as an argument for the validity of a position or the soundness of a principle." As Gabriel succinctly put it, "The implication always is that, if Lincoln so believed, the matter is closed."[1] Conspicuous among the examples cited was President Franklin D. Roosevelt's use of the Great Emancipator.

During the same years of revived interest in the national heritage, another student of American culture, Dixon Wecter, had essayed the same subject from a somewhat different perspective. The fruit of his inquiry, entitled *The Hero in America*, was published in 1941. Its subtitle—*A Chronicle of Hero-Worship*—suggested the nature of the approach. A closing chapter on Franklin D. Roosevelt not only testified that the incumbent President had already established himself among popular immortals ranging from George Washington to Buffalo Bill, but also revealed that he had done some hero-worshipping of his own. Exploring Roosevelt's uses of history, Wecter showed how the President had exploited analogies with two of his predecessors in his two succeeding administrations.

> The tutelary genius of Roosevelt's first term might have been Jefferson, a bookish liberal who proved, as the squire of Hyde Park remarked at Monticello, that it is possible for a great gentleman to be a great commoner. The genius of the second term, at least at its beginning, seemed to be the more pugnacious democrat from the Hermitage. On Election Day, 1936, for luck, Roosevelt wore Jackson's heavy gold watch-chain. . . .At subsequent Jackson Day dinners Mr. Roosevelt himself has suggested the parallel, and he provided that the reviewing stand for the 1937 inaugural parade should be a replica of the Hermitage.[2]

"Only Lincoln, greatest of war Presidents," Wecter concluded on a note of anticipation, "was left for purpose of analogy." Indeed, the Democratic chief executive had already acknowledged parallels with the Republican crisis President.

2

"When I became President I found a country demoralized,

disorganized . . . ," Franklin Roosevelt declared in a 1938 campaign speech. "As in the time of George Washington in 1787, when there was grave danger that the states would never become a Nation—as in the time of Abraham Lincoln, when a tragic division threatened to become lasting—our own time has brought a test to our American Union." Like his eminent predecessors, Roosevelt had met the challenge of disunity. "A great part of my duty as President has been to do what I could to bring our people together again."[3]

Although the political manipulation of the Lincoln image only reached its culmination late in Franklin Roosevelt's second presidential term, it had figured in the rhetoric and ceremony of the preceding years, as Ralph Henry Gabriel acknowledged. The factors compelling an alliance between the Great Emancipator and the New Deal President were not hard to discern. Long before the international crises of the late Thirties, Roosevelt had found a potent parallel to the Depression in the secession crisis which faced Lincoln when he entered the White House. Moreover, for a leader who sought to identify with the common man and appeal to the independent voter, a claim to the Lincoln succession followed logically. Accordingly, Roosevelt frequently wrapped himself in the mantle of the Civil War President.

As early as April 3, 1929, the newly inaugurated Governor of New York had anticipated the future use of the Great Emancipator. "I think it is time for us Democrats to claim Lincoln as one of our own," Roosevelt wrote to the Jefferson biographer, Claude Bowers. "The Republican Party has certainly repudiated, first and last, everything that he stood for."[4] Five years later, in his second "Fireside Chat" of 1934, the President invoked the magic name to counter attacks on the New Deal recovery programs. "I believe with Abraham Lincoln, that 'The legitimate object of government is to do for a community of people whatever they need to have done but cannot do at all or cannot do so well for themselves in their separate and individual capacities.' "[5] The Republican President's words seemed so pertinent to the New Deal that Roosevelt repeated them on at least two other occasions.

Making a pilgrimage to the birthplace of the Great Emancipator in the spring of 1936—itself an unthinkable gesture for a Democratic executive in earlier years—Roosevelt emerged from the restored cabin with "a renewed confidence that the spirit of America is not dead, that men and means will be found to explore and conquer the problems of a new time with no less humanity and no less fortitude than his. Here," he declared, "we can renew our pledge of fidelity to the faith which Lincoln held in the common man. . . ." When he could find historical precedents for his programs, the President exploited them. In defending his plan to reorganize the federal judiciary in a 1937 radio broadcast, Roosevelt reminded his listeners that some of his illustrious predecessors, including Abraham Lincoln, had also called upon Congress to reform the bench.[6]

The following year, the Democratic President made even more potent use of the Lincoln image. Addressing some of his most ardent supporters on "the basic morals of democracy," Roosevelt placed himself in direct line of descent. "Let me talk history," he began, and proceeded to call the roll of Presidents who had battled for "government . . . responsive to the public will" against "the small minority that claimed vested rights to power." Along with the customary Democratic stalwarts, the President named Lincoln as well as his own dynamic cousin. In 1904, he recalled, "I voted for . . . Theodore Roosevelt because I thought he was a better Democrat than the Democratic candidate." The same, presumably, went for the Great Emancipator. "Lincoln, too, fought for the morals of democracy," Roosevelt declared, and then deftly separated the first Republican President from his party contemporaries, "—and had he lived the south would have been allowed to rehabilitate itself of the basis of those morals instead of being 'reconstructed' by martial law and carpetbaggers." It only remained for the President to add that "this Administration seeks to serve the needs, and to make effective the will, of the overwhelming majority of our citizens and seeks to curb only abuses of power and privilege by small minorities. Thus," Roosevelt concluded, "we in turn are striving to uphold the integrity of the morals of our democracy."[7] Which, in his time, meant the New Deal program.

That summer Roosevelt renewed the same theme before an altogether different audience of some 150,000. Dedicating the Gettysburg Memorial on the anniversary of the famous battle, once more he sought parallels between himself and the Civil War President. "It seldom helps to wonder how a statesman of one generation would surmount the crisis of another," Roosevelt admitted. "But the fullness of the stature of Lincoln's nature and the fundamental conflict which events forced upon his Presidency, invite us ever to turn to him for help." Besides, the issue restated in the Gettysburg Address would ever confront "the Nation so long as we cling to the purposes for which the Nation was founded—to preserve under the changing conditions of each generation a people's government for the people's good." Though the tasks might change, the challenge would remain the same. Now Americans faced it once more, Roosevelt concluded,

> a conflict as fundamental as Lincoln's, fought not with glint of steel, but with appeals to reason and justice on a thousand fronts—seeking to save for our common country opportunity and security for citizens in a free society.
>   We are near to winning this battle. In its winning and through the years may we live by the wisdom and the humanity of the heart of Abraham Lincoln.[8]

Such studied references by the President inevitably prompted others to take up the parallels. In his popular 1938 biography of Roosevelt, Emil Ludwig dwelt on the "com-

parison with Lincoln." "The characters—profoundly different. . . . And yet," he continued, "they are linked by two
immense qualities, humor and friendliness. When I asked
Roosevelt what Lincoln meant to him he gave me, without a
moment's hesitation, this answer: 'Lincoln? The greatest
humanitarian!' " "My respect for Emil Ludwig ran higher on
seeing the work he did with you," the Lincoln biographer
Carl Sandburg wrote the President. The humanitarianism
which Roosevelt had stressed also impressed Max Lerner.
Reviewing the published messages of the President, the liberal
journalist declared: "The needs and hungers and aspirations
of the ordinary man and woman speak, in all their confusion,
through these volumes as they have never spoken before in
the state papers of an American President since Lincoln." But
Roosevelt's erstwhile Brain Truster. Raymond Moley, had
heard enough of the "new clichés" like the proposition
"that Roosevelt is greater than Abraham Lincoln." He exag-
gerated, of course. The journalist Richard Neuberger recorded a much more common reaction when he quoted a
wheat farmer in the Pacific Northwest: "Our President is the
greatest President since Lincoln."[9]

Long before Roosevelt, in concluding his 1939 Message to
Congress, prophesied that his generation would "nobly
save . . . the last best hope of earth," Republicans had grown
indignant at the President's repeated use of the Lincoln
idiom. Yet not one of them had risen to contend with the
interloper. Finally, ex-President Hoover, the New Deal's most
redoubtable critic, responded at a Lincoln Day banquet the
following month. Recently, both Roosevelt and Communist
boss Earl Browder had claimed Lincoln "as a founder of their
faiths," Hoover observed, adding disdainfully: "I was under
the impression he was a Republican." "Whatever this New
Deal system is, it is certain that it did not come from
Abraham Lincoln," the Republican elder statesman declared,
launching into an extended discourse on their incompati-

bility. The liberty the Great Emancipator fought for had nothing in common with the current Democratic perversion.[10]

If the Great Engineer remained convinced that "the spirit of Abraham Lincoln has not joined the New Deal," some of his opponents claimed the very opposite. And though Roosevelt still refrained from explicitly enrolling the Great Emancipator in the Democratic ranks, some of his supporters showed no such restraint. The most outspoken claims had come from the floor of the House of Representatives on Lincoln's birthday, 1936. There, Congressman Frank Dorsey of Pennsylvania exploited the parallels between the issues of the Depression and the Civil War. "Lincoln was the progressive, the new dealer of his day," he exclaimed. "If he were alive now he would discern that economic peonage is as terrible a thing as the selling of men on the block." In Dorsey's view, Lincoln's concept of liberty hardly squared with that of the Du Ponts and the Liberty League—or, by extension, with that described by Herbert Hoover two years later. "Because he abhorred the thought of precious human beings becoming mere chattel," the Congressman concluded, Lincoln "would have been one of our leaders. As a present-day Democrat, I salute the man who saw eye-to-eye with us. . . ."[11]

Lagging prudently behind his more enthusiastic supporters in Congress, Roosevelt nevertheless moved toward the same conclusion. His first objective on the way, however, was to deny the contemporary Republican Party any claim to Lincoln. In the fraternal atmosphere of successive Jackson Day dinners, the President skillfully drove a wedge between Father Abraham and his political progeny. "In these recent years the average American seldom thinks of Jefferson and Jackson as Democrats or of Lincoln and Theodore Roosevelt as Republicans," he declared in 1938. Instead, "he labels each one of them according to his attitude toward the

fundamental problems that confronted him as President. . . ."
Lincoln, like the rest, in Roosevelt's view, had fought the
very minority class privilege against which he now inveighed.
The following year, in the same sanctuary, Roosevelt asked
the rhetorical question: "Does anyone maintain that the
Republican Party from 1868 to 1938 . . . was the party of
Abraham Lincoln? To claim that is . . . absurd." At the 1940
Democratic "love feast," he completed the process by lodg-
ing common claim to the Civil War President.

> I do not know which party Lincoln would belong to if he were
> alive in 1940—and I am not even concerned to speculate on it; a
> new party had to be created before he could be elected President.
> I am more interested in the fact that he did the big job which
> then had to be done—to preserve the Union and make possible, at
> a later time, the united country that we all live in today. His
> sympathies and his motives of championship of humanity itself
> have made him for all centuries to come the legitimate property
> of all parties—of every man and woman and child in every part of
> our land.[12]

It was a fitting preface to a political campaign which would
see the Democratic candidate for President take full possession of the symbol of the Republican birthright.

Fiorello La Guardia, the maverick Republican mayor of
New York, embraced the same theme on Lincoln's birthday
when he predicted that "seventy-five years from today, our
present President, Franklin Delano Roosevelt, will be hailed
as a liberator just as we are hailing Lincoln."[13]

In early June of the election year, Roosevelt played host
to leaders of the American Youth Congress, fresh from the
campuses where disenchantment with the President ran high.
Questions and challenges filled the air of the crowded East
Room. The old guns or butter dilemma recurred: why had he
sacrificed the New Deal for preparedness? Roosevelt pointedly reached back into history for his answer. "Have you read
Carl Sandburg's *Lincoln*?" he asked, and then continued:

> I think the impression was that Lincoln was a pretty sad man, because he could not do all he wanted to do at one time, and I think you will find examples where Lincoln had to compromise to gain a little something. He had to compromise to make a few gains. Lincoln was one of those unfortunate people called a "politician" but he was a politician who was practical enough to get a great many things for his country. He was a sad man because he couldn't get it all at once. And nobody can.[14]

No one could fail to grasp the lesson—or the speaker's studied effort to identify his predicament with that of his famous predecessor.

In 1939, Max Lerner had heralded "a new and revived Lincoln image in the making" as "almost providentially made for our present national crisis." A year later, he linked it with the incumbent President. Though writing even before the party conventions, Lerner had no doubt that the "crisis President" would be renominated and reelected at a time of deepest national difficulty. "Roosevelt has always had a sense of history," he remarked.

> One thing Roosevelt has said clearly: he has no intention of being another Buchanan. Which implies that all the basic conditions that characterize a country on the eve of a civil war are true of our period. But to avoid being a Buchanan in the face of impending civil war one must be something of a Lincoln. How much of Lincoln does Roosevelt have in him? More, I am convinced, than any President since Lincoln or before.[15]

3

As the 1940 presidential campaign entered its later stages, the author of *Abe Lincoln in Illinois*, that popular combination of legend and lesson which had effectively focused the search for a usable past upon one man, joined the President's staff. Eleanor Roosevelt had seen Robert Sherwood's play at its pre-Broadway premiere in Washington. "Strange, how fundamentally people seem to have fought on much the same

issues throughout our history!" she observed in a congratula-
tory letter to the dramatist. Characteristically, the First Lady
had then shared her enthusiasm with everyone from her
husband to the countless readers of her syndicated newspaper
column, "My Day." After seeing the film version, President
Roosevelt wrote the playwright requesting a copy of the two
Lincoln speeches delivered in the debate scene. In a letter
accompanying the transcripts, Sherwood repeated what he
had recently told Harry Hopkins: "I wish with all my heart
to offer my services, for whatever they're worth, to you in
this crucial year and to the cause which is yours as surely as it
was Lincoln's."[16] A few months later he received a call.

In the first days of October, Roosevelt's chief speech
writer, Samuel Rosenman, asked Hopkins to help him "cast
about" for some "new blood" to fortify his team. Hopkins
mentioned his friend Sherwood. "I had met him personally
only once . . . ," Rosenman recalled years later; "but I was,
of course, familiar with his plays. I said that his plays certainly indicated a liberal point of view, and that his activities
on the Committee to Defend America by Aiding the Allies
showed that he shared the President's views on foreign
policy." Shortly afterward, Hopkins brought Sherwood over
to Rosenman's New York apartment. "At first, I did not
know why I was there," Sherwood later confessed; "but I
soon found out that I had been pressed into service as a
'ghost writer.' . . ." Indeed, his employment commenced immediately as Rosenman set him to work on the President's
Columbus Day address to the Americas, to be delivered at
Dayton, Ohio a few days later. "From that moment on,"
Sherwood recollected with lingering astonishment, "for the
next five years, Hopkins, Rosenman and I worked closely
together on all the major Roosevelt speeches until the President's death."[17]

In such a way, the Lincoln playwright had joined the
presidential staff; in time he became Rosenman's favorite

collaborator. "He was an excellent judge of the effect of words upon audiences—he had become one of the leading dramatists . . . partly because of that ability," according to the presidential aide. "He was a burning enthusiast for the New Deal and for a strong international policy; if anything, he had to be restrained rather than encouraged." Sherwood quickly submerged his own personality in the President's, however, and the speeches rarely bore marks of his authorship. In part, Roosevelt's own final revisions accounted for the uniform character and style in his addresses. Moreover, Sherwood quickly developed an uncanny feeling for the President's mind and role. "In the end no one understood Franklin better than he," Rexford Tugwell observed years later.[18]

Less than two weeks after Sherwood joined the speech-writing staff, the Lincoln name and words appeared in a Roosevelt address. In the latter part of October, Roosevelt set out for Philadelphia for the formal opening of the campaign he had been waging for months. The presidential train paused long enough in Delaware, home of the conservative Du Pont family, for the candidate to deliver some terse remarks. "Four years ago Wilmington was the home town of the famous Liberty League," he pointedly observed. At that time, it seemed "a good place to read from a speech" in which Abraham Lincoln defined "liberty" as the right of "each man to do as he pleases with himself, and the product of his labor. . . ." In 1936, Roosevelt had aligned himself with his Republican predecessor in the battle against economic bondage. Furthermore, by reelecting him that year, the President suggested, the voters had rejected the reactionary Liberty League. Now that the march of totalitarianism abroad had extended the issue of liberty beyond the national boundaries, Roosevelt hoped the electorate would reaffirm its earlier decision. "I am sure," he knowingly concluded, "that this year the people, not only of Delaware but of the

United States, are all taking a renewed interest in that word 'liberty.' "[19]

The next evening, in a radio address closing the *New York Herald Tribune* Forum, "Saving Democracy," the President again took a Lincoln text. Once more he sought parallels to illuminate and vindicate the Administration foreign policy. In his famed Cooper Institute speech, Lincoln had warned his audience against, as Roosevelt put it, "the fear-mongers and the calamity howlers—the 'appeasers' of that troubled time, appeasers who were numerous and influential." The President admonished his own listeners to reaffirm Lincoln's declaration of faith today. "It gives the right answer—the American answer—to the foreign propagandists who seek to divide us with their strategy of terror." Roosevelt considered the words so compelling that he repeated them at the conclusion of his remarks.

> We have confidence in the ability of the democratic system which gives men dignity, to give them strength. And so we say with Lincoln: "Let us have faith that right makes might, and in that faith let us to the end dare to do our duty as we understand it."[20]

Two weeks away from the climax of his grueling campaign for the Presidency, Wendell Willkie, the Republican nominee, paused in Springfield, Illinois—traditional hallowed ground of his party. But even there Abraham Lincoln was no longer the special property of the GOP. "Within the last year and a half," Willkie complained, "the candidate for the third term as President . . . has made speeches in which he has inferentially described himself as Washington, Jefferson, Lincoln, Cleveland, Wilson and Theodore Roosevelt." Such comparisons, however, served no useful purpose; neither of the candidates, the Republican standard-bearer admitted, was a great man. "Neither of us has demonstrated any of the qualities of greatness demonstrated by Washington or Lincoln. . . ."[21] Lacking even an echo of Herbert Hoover's forlorn attempt to make the Great Emancipator into a modern Republican, Willkie's was a curiously negative performance. At the home of the man whose life and death "made him the symbol, the hope, and the purpose of America," the Republican candidate limited his remarks to a denial of Roosevelt's claim to succession.

4

The very presence of Robert Sherwood on the White House staff helped to cement the identification of Roosevelt with the renewed Lincoln image of the period. But Sherwood remained only the author of *Abe Lincoln in Illinois.* The role of the new incarnation of the Great Emancipator fell upon the star of the drama, Raymond Massey—a Roosevelt supporter—and perhaps even more profoundly, upon Carl Sandburg. With the publication of *The Prairie Years*, the Chicago poet had gained widespread attention. The ensuing, extended years of well publicized labor on its sequel— interrupted by appearances as a vagabond minstrel on the lecture circuit—had furthered his place as a homespun interpreter of the American heritage. In the eyes of a segment of the public—typified by the untold legion of high school English teachers who enshrined *The Prairie Years* alongside *John Brown's Body*—he gradually became a positive national institution.

With the publication of *The War Years*, Sandburg's inheritance was assured. "How inextricably your name will be linked to Lincoln's in the years to come," exclaimed his friend the editor William Allen White. A host of honorary degrees the following spring paid tribute to Sandburg's achievement as a biographer while the citations often testified to the growing identification of the author with his subject. Harvard dubbed him "the Washington correspondent

of the Lincoln administration," and Yale declared that "Carl
Sandburg will live with his hero, and deserves to, not only
because of his researches but because he himself illustrates his
hero's qualities—simplicity, humor and love of humanity." [22]

Every such salute contributed indirectly to the Roosevelt
campaign, for Sandburg made no secret of his support for the
Democratic candidate. While maintaining the guise of an
independent, he had voted for Roosevelt in each election.
More important, he had been quick to compare the President
with Abraham Lincoln. "I see many striking parallels between Lincoln and Franklin Roosevelt," Carl Sandburg wrote
Raymond Moley only seven months after the first inauguration. The poet even suggested that he might fashion an article
along such lines for Moley's new magazine, *Today*.
"Lincoln—Roosevelt," which appeared early in 1934, concentrated upon a single comparison. To Sandburg, the labor
provisions of Roosevelt's NRA represented nothing less than
a second Emancipation Proclamation. "Those who live by
selling their labor . . . are having their status changed," the
Lincoln authority concluded. Occupied with his long Civil
War biography, Sandburg still found no escape from the
present. "I have my eyes and ears in two eras and cannot help
drawing parallels," the poet admitted in a flattering letter to
the President in 1935. "One runs to the effect that you are
the best light of democracy that has occupied the White
House since Lincoln." Even more important, "as with
Lincoln there has been a response of the People to you: they
have done something to you and made you what you could
not have been without them, this interplay operating steadily
in your growth." In 1936, Sandburg took time off to deliver
four campaign speeches exploiting contemporary parallels
with the election of 1864, to the incumbent's benefit. Writing in *The New Republic* at the same time, he termed
Roosevelt "a momentous historic character . . . thoroughly
aware of what he is doing and where he is going. . . ."[23]

In 1940, it momentarily appeared that the now legendary Lincoln interpreter might himself become a candidate in the election. When word that Sandburg was considering running for the House of Representatives reached Washington, the President responded with enthusiasm. "I sincerely hope the rumor is true," he wrote, "—incidentally, I have a real belief that you could win and it would be grand to have your kind of Lincoln liberal in the Congress." [24] Even more startling was a brief flurry of interest in Sandburg as the Republican presidential nominee. But here too the poet's own sense of his limitations, coupled with the cold-blooded calculations of the party professionals, put a stop to the political sentimentalism.

Even such abortive booms emphasized the prominent standing of the man most clearly identified with Lincoln. Sandburg's rise had accompanied the rediscovery of the folk figure hidden inside the Civil War President and he took advantage of the circumstance as he stumped for Roosevelt. In a speech entitled "What Lincoln Would Have Done," he insisted simply that the Great Emancipator would have done exactly what Roosevelt was doing.

On election eve, the Democrats went on the air, coast-to-coast, for two final hours of campaigning. Short speeches by the President, Secretary of State Hull, Alexander Woollcott, and Dorothy Thompson alternated with Broadway and Hollywood entertainment as an estimated 80 million Americans tuned in. Finally, for the climactic five minutes of the broadcast, Carl Sandburg came on, speaking for the independent voters of the country. The Midwestern twang of his voice hung in the midnight air as he recalled once again the critical presidential election of 1864. Then the independent voters had come to the support of the lonely man in the White House. Tomorrow they would speak once more. Sandburg read a lengthy excerpt from an obscure Presbyterian minister's estimate of Lincoln. The words sounded curiously appropriate on the poet's lips.

> The explanation of his every act is this: He executes the will of
> the people. . . . His wisdom consists in carrying out the good
> sense of the nation. His growth in political knowledge, his steady
> movement . . . are but the growth and movement of the national
> mind. . . . He stands before you . . . a not perfect man and yet
> more precious than fine gold.

"And for some of us," the Lincoln biographer concluded,
"that goes, in the main, in the present hour of national fate,
for Franklin Delano Roosevelt."[25]

5

Stephen Vincent Benét also made his contribution, albeit
in a characteristically lower key, to the creation of a Lincoln
presence during the final hours of the 1940 presidential
campaign. On election day, the *New York Post's* F. P. A.
published a new poem by Benét. Entitled "Tuesday, November
5th, 1940," it purported to represent the collective voice
of "the people" speaking out in behalf of Franklin Roosevelt.
But the poem emerged also as a tribute and appeal to their
loyalty and something of a New Deal valedictory. Once again
the story of a government of compassion, touching the lives
of common individuals everywhere, was recounted: "our
kids, growing up with a chance"; "the old folks who don't
have to go to the poorhouse"; and "the tanned faces of the
boys from the CCC." Others, "the wise guys," might now
disregard their debt to the New Deal, but "We remember,
F.D.R." The people had not forgotten their leader.

"Now there's another election," Benét continued in the
collective idiom, moving toward his conclusion.

> And they say you don't know the people.
> And they say you want to be a dictator
>   . . .
> In fact, to tell you a secret, they say you're terrible.

And, if I may speak from the record, we know them, too.
And that's jake with us.
It's jake with us, because we know.
And we know you never were a Fuehrer and never will be,
Not a Fuehrer, just a guy in pitching for the bunch of us,
For all of us, the whole people.
A big guy pitching, with America in his heart.
A man who knows the tides and ways of the people
As Abe Lincoln knew the wind on the prairies,
And has never once stopped believing in them.
(The slow, tenacious memory of the people,
Somehow, holding on to the Lincolns, no matter who yelled
  against them . . .)

A country squire from Hyde Park with a Harvard accent,
Who never once failed the people
And whom the people won't fail.[26]

On the evening after the presidential election, Raymond
Massey stood on the stage of Carnegie Hall and read a
nonpartisan appeal for national unity which Stephen Vincent
Benét had written at the behest of the Council for Democracy. "This campaign has been a very bitter one. We had
better face that fact and admit it. . . ," said the familiar voice
over a million radios. "In ordinary times, that doesn't matter
so much," the actor continued. But these were "not ordinary
times because there is a crisis in our national life." Ominous
events across the seas had driven Americans to rearm: their
precious way of life might no longer go unchallenged. But the
issue encompassed more than military preparedness. How
might all Americans defend the liberty and democracy which
the election of the preceding day had once more dramatized?
"We know one thing," he replied. "—Abraham Lincoln said it
more than eighty years ago. . . . He said: 'A house divided
against itself cannot stand.' We cannot be a house divided—
divided in will, divided in interest, divided in soul. We cannot
be a house divided and live."[27]

Americans must now discard their partisanships, no matter
how inflamed. Characteristically, Benét turned to American

history for precedent. "We have a great past to help us, in putting these things aside," read the actor who had become the popular personification of Lincoln. After the bitter struggle between Jefferson and Hamilton, after the bitter strife of the Civil War, Americans had reunited to sustain their common nation. "Let us be bold enough and free enough to follow the great examples," Massey intoned "—the men of good will and honor who put aside little ways and petty hatreds to build the American dream."[28],

The next day, *The New York Times* carried the story on page one, headed "Lincoln-like plea of Benét sounds keynote. . . ." Pronouncing the appeal the "most impressive presentation" of the evening, the reporter dwelt on the Lincolnian character of both the speech and its delivery. Benét had employed simple words, as if to imitate the style of the Great Emancipator. And Raymond Massey had responded to the spirit of the piece. "As he began to read," the story related, "his tones were those of an ordinary American of 1940, but as he progressed the almost sing-song delivery of his Lincoln crept upon him, and soon he was using with complete naturalness the careless country-man speech of the Lincoln of the play."[29]

The presidential election of 1940 marked a turning point in the political uses of the Lincoln image. The campaign witnessed the final attempt by the President and liberals such as Sherwood, Sandburg, and Benét to link the Great Emancipator with Administration domestic policies. By November, international questions occupied the writers who supported Roosevelt. In the face of fascist aggression abroad, they advocated aid to the democratic allies who resisted it. Accordingly, they no longer directed their verbal volleys at the remnants of the Liberty League, but at the isolationists now rallying under the America First banner. Far from abandoning the search for a usable past, Sherwood, Sandburg, and Benét made it the foundation of their interventionist plat-

form. Indeed, in seeking to link their candidate's program of
aid to the Allies with the Lincoln tradition, they found
support in the commitment to the universal defense of
democracy which the Great Emancipator had enunciated at
Gettysburg. Perhaps Sherwood expressed the new conception
of Lincoln best in early 1939: "he seemed to have a breadth
of view which encompassed the whole human race; he
seemed to feel that the American people had an obligation to
their fellow men everywhere to prove that democracy can
live and grow."[30]   That usable past provided a basis for a
program to defend democracy wherever it was threatened.

chapter six

WILLIAM ALLEN WHITE AND
AN INTERVENTIONIST LINCOLN

1

By the end of 1940, with the help of two poets and especially the playwright who had recently joined his staff, President Roosevelt had successfully molded a modern Lincoln
image for his own political purposes. His use of the Lincoln
name and idiom to legitimize the New Deal had become a
commonplace. In large measure, the enlistment of the Lincoln symbol under the New Deal banner had served an
exclusive purpose: to demonstrate that the Democratic Party
alone stood in direct line of descent from a great American
tradition. Domestic issues perforce remained partisan. To
transfer the Lincoln sanction to a foreign policy position
required molding it into an inclusive symbol to serve a
primarily nonpartisan purpose.

It was essential, then, that the Lincoln mantle become the
possession, too, of a Republican supporter of the Roosevelt
diplomacy. An unlikely figure emerged to claim the emblem:
William Allen White, rotund editor of the *Emporia Gazette*.
Perhaps more than anyone else, he became identified with aid
to the Allies, so much so that the leading American interven-

tionist organization popularly bore his name. At the same time, his leadership of public opinion campaigns in support of the President's foreign policy brought the two men closer together.

White became identified with the Great Emancipator in four ways. First, his own background and character lent themselves to such comparison. Second, he employed the Lincoln idiom in his own part of the campaign for aid to the Allies. Third, his activities brought him into collaboration with Roosevelt, Sherwood, and others who, while also linked with Lincoln, supported a similar foreign policy. Finally, White and his cause benefited when the leading spokesman for isolation, Charles Lindbergh, inadvertently placed himself in thorough opposition to their Lincolnian precepts.

2

The similarity between Lincoln and White included the superficial elements of common Midwestern background and grass roots identification. Social class orientation represented a more important factor. On the day of Lincoln's funeral, Emerson, summing up, had declared that at last this "middle-class country had got a middle-class president. . . ." In his own time, White had become the folk hero of the same segment of society. Even an eastern metropolitan vehicle like *The New York Times* admitted it, calling him the "incarnate voice of the American middle class."

An even deeper tie bound the newspaper editor to the Great Emancipator. Lincoln epitomized the genius of the Republican Party, to which White maintained a steadfast loyalty throughout the years following his youthful participation in the Bull Moose revolt. According to his foremost biographer, White considered himself "a Lincolnesque type of Republican, interested in the Republican party as the

party of the people and not the party of the selfish rich."
Throughout the Depression decade, the editor sought to
remind his party of its Lincolnian heritage. "Go to the
people, Mr. President," he urged the hapless Hoover in an
editorial late in 1930. "They are dependable. Lincoln, Roosevelt and Wilson found the people a tower of refuge and of
strength. Whoever is wise and honest and brave, they will
follow to victory." His sense of that heritage and his progressive persuasion committed White to seek a positive Republican alternative to the New Deal. "If the Republican
party has the courage to turn to the humanity of Lincoln and
away from the property-minded leadership which has dominated it most of the time for 20 years," he wired the
Associated Press in 1935, "we can save America. But America
cannot be saved by merely denouncing the faults of Roosevelt." In order to register his enduring disdain for the Old
Guard, which, in his view, perverted Republican Party purposes, the Kansas editor enlivened the AP and UP wires
during the stagnant summer of 1937 with the sincere but
impious declaration that insurgent New York Mayor Fiorello
La Guardia alone met the GOP leadership requirements. He
was their "Modern Lincoln." Next day, while party elders
exploded in outrage, the Mayor quipped: "This is the first
kind word I have heard from a Republican in a long time."[1]

"Will White had the same instincts as Lincoln," declared
David Hinshaw in the first of the posthumous biographies.
"He was a man of the people, as was Lincoln. . . ." During
the last years of his life, when war raged in much of the
world, others linked the editor's name with that of the Great
Emancipator. Responding to White's enthusiastic tribute to
The War Years, Carl Sandburg expressed his gratification in
knowing that the book was "out there in your house where
the Lincoln tradition has had such rare loyalty." In 1940,
V. Y. Dallman exclaimed, "He is as Lincolnlike as a mortal
can be, except in his style of architecture!" in a Lincoln's

birthday piece for the *Illinois Register*.[2]

Though a Republican and a frequent critic of the New Deal domestic programs, White early registered his support of Roosevelt's foreign policy. Only two months after the first inauguration, the Emporian observed in an editorial that the President was apparently "preparing to cut away from the ancient tradition which provided for the isolation of America." The editor immediately signaled his approval: "The GAZETTE has believed for fifteen years that isolation is impossible for any nation that takes leadership in a modern world. The GAZETTE believed in the Wilsonian idea. We welcome the Rooseveltian attitude."[3] Throughout the years of Roosevelt leadership, White continued steadfastly to support the Administration foreign policy.

3

In the autumn of 1939, internationalists on the eastern seaboard sought a chairman for their nascent Non-Partisan Committee for Peace through Revision of the Neutrality Law. Almost as though it were 1860, they turned to a Midwestern Republican to rally the country—and especially the pivotal Heartland—behind the President's program to repeal the arms embargo provisions. The selection of William Allen White also gratified the Administration; indeed, Secretary of State Cordell Hull had first suggested his name.

In only a month the Committee completed its assignment to mobilize public opinion behind the amending legislation. Even in his brief tenure, however, White established a reputation as a leading spokesman for a bipartisan internationalist foreign policy and showed a proclivity to view the issues in idealistic terms. He displayed this latter tendency in his major address of the crusade, broadcast over the Columbia radio network on October 15. True to his lights, White denied that

the war "is . . . a contest of imperialist nations struggling for
place and power. It is a clash of ideologies," he asserted.
"The struggle of two thousand years for human liberty has
been wiped out east of the Rhine. . . ." The European democracies "are carrying our banner, fighting the American battle," the editor declared in calling upon his audience not to
deny the Allies the "arms and materials" needed to defend
"our common cause." Shortly afterward, Carl Sandburg
wrote White that "you have a Lincoln manner of saying
terrible things so gently that the reader goes back to make
sure."[4]

The Lincoln motif was more pronounced in *Defense for
America*, a volume of internationalist essays by fourteen
prominent Americans, which White edited the following winter. While his contributors employed a variety of interventionist arguments, the editor in an introduction prepared
shortly before the collection went to press, characteristically
concentrated upon the moral issues at stake. What he saw
threatened by European dictators was more than American
security. It was a philosophy of life which had been gradually
framed over two millennia and now undergirded the western
social order. In his mind, "that democratic sense of truth and
beauty which men call freedom is what the gun and tank, the
flame and their horrendous bomb are challenging today."[5]

To thrive at home, the democratic idea must be defended
abroad. The Emporia editor's vision bore such kinship with
Lincoln's that his words formed a paraphrase of the Great
Emancipator's.

> The two philosophies—the philosophy of force and tyranny, and
> the philosophy of neighborly kindliness that we call democracy—
> cannot meet and mingle on the same planet! The world has
> shrunken. Our great round earth with its vast ocean and wide land
> has been drawn together with machinery until it is a little place, a
> veritable neighborhood that *cannot live half slave and half free*.

Viewed in White's terms, the war became a veritable world

struggle, with American front line trenches everywhere that freedom was threatened. "[W]hoever challenges man's liberty," he proclaimed, "wherever he is, is our enemy. Wherever a free man is in chains we are threatened also. Whoever is fighting for liberty is defending America."[6]

4

Idealistic words sufficed during the winter of the so-called phony war. But the Nazi blitzkrieg in the spring brought White back into action—this time as head of a new committee to awaken and align public opinion behind a program of aid to the faltering democracies of Europe. Quickly the organizers ignited a brushfire of concern that flashed across the country. A flurry of telegrams to influential citizens brought a prompt and heartening response. On May 20 William Allen White announced the formation of the Committee to Defend America by Aiding the Allies. The news stirred the grassroots. Within six weeks, 300 local committees had been formed. One contributing factor to this growth was the conspicuous association of White's name with the organization.

In the following months, the editor from Emporia worked closely with Robert Sherwood, one of the most active leaders of the Committee, and Franklin Roosevelt, who enthusiastically cooperated with the organization, in quest of their common goals. But White lent more than his name and personal contacts to the Committee. He spoke out in print and on the platform, investing the cause with a moral fervor which frequently found expression in the same words of Lincoln, "half slave and half free," that he had used in *Defense for America*. The editor even repeated the phrase over nationwide radio. On August 22, at the height of the Committee's campaign in support of the proposed destroyers-for-bases exchange, White delivered an address over the CBS

network. While others debated the legal, military, and diplomatic dimensions of the issue, the Sage of Emporia once
more emphasized the moral. "If Great Britain falls," he
warned

> a new phase of civilization will dominate Europe and will menace
> the United States and the Western Hemisphere. It is not a ques-
> tion of form of government between Great Britain and the
> European dictators. It is a way of thinking, a way of life, a social
> order, a slave economy that menaces the world, and the world
> cannot live half slave and half free.[7]

During the eventful days of mid-1940, William Allen White
had made certain that the familiar words of Lincoln rang in
the air, reviving a determined and heroic past while conjuring
up implications for the present. Whatever else, no one could
fail to grasp the sense of implacable antagonism to tyranny
which the phrase carried for the speaker. Like the Lincoln of
folklore, White could not compromise with those who en-
slaved their fellow men.

William Allen White also cooperated increasingly with the
President. "I always conferred with him on our program,"
the chairman recalled afterward. Invariably, "our program"
coincided with the objectives of Administration policy, so the
two leaders coordinated their activities. That the success of
their separate efforts depended, similarly, on public opinion
also brought them together. On June 10, the day Mussolini
opportunistically declared war on France, White wired the
President: "My correspondence is heaping up unanimously
behind the plan to aid the Allies by anything other than war.
As an old friend, let me warn you that maybe you will not be
able to lead the American people unless you catch up with
them. They are going fast."[8]

As if in reply, the President overtook his countrymen in a
commencement address at the University of Virginia the very
same day. Roosevelt eloquently condemned the action of the
Italian government: "the hand that held the dagger has struck

it into the back of its neighbor." More important, he enunciated the sweeping foreign policy that White and many Americans had been demanding. Calling the isolationist dream of an island America "a helpless nightmare," the President outlined a program of economic intervention: "we will extend to the opponents of force the material resources of this nation; and at the same time, we will harness and speed up the use of those resources in order that we ourselves in the Americas may have equipment and training equal to the task of any emergency and every defense."[9] Despite isolated exceptions to both the insult to Il Duce and the new policy, Americans in general welcomed and rallied behind the address, as William Allen White had predicted.

Twice during the summer of 1940, White sought to perform vital and timely services for the Chief Executive. In the first he succeeded. Shortly after the President named Henry L. Stimson Secretary of War and Frank Knox Secretary of the Navy, the editor arrived in Washington to commend the appointment of the prominent Republican internationalists to the cabinet. Immediately, Roosevelt confided his anxiety about Senate confirmation. At his host's request, White secured the names of doubtful Senators and then persuaded influential constituents to bombard them with telegrams until the appointments were approved.

White's second attempt to assist the President, however, met with very little success. While the Committee to Defend America by Aiding the Allies lobbied for the release of fifty overaged American destroyers to the depleted British navy, Roosevelt chafed over the political price of such a measure. Defeat of the proposal would represent a setback for his reelection campaign. Thus, before proceeding, the Administration wanted the GOP candidate, Wendell Willkie, to signal his support by rallying Republicans in Congress behind the plan. William Allen White sought a somewhat less ambitious goal: a joint statement in favor of assistance by the two party leaders. Failing that, however, he could only deliver private assurances that Willkie would not publicly attack the transaction. Roosevelt eventually bypassed the Congress altogether, concluding the destroyers-for-bases deal by executive agreement.

When, after the election of 1940, the President moved even farther toward intervention, William Allen White registered his strong support. In response to urgent British pleas for more aid, Roosevelt went on the air two days before the end of the year. Employing the fireside chat format, he exploited parallels with his informal message on the banking crisis of 1933. In the major part of his address to the nation, the President urged a program of unlimited and unconditional aid to the Allies based on the conviction that "there is far less chance of the United States getting into war" if we support the enemies of the Axis. "The people of Europe who are defending themselves do not ask us to do their fighting," Roosevelt assured his listeners. "They ask us for the implements of war, the planes, the tanks, the guns, the freighters which will enable them to fight for their liberty and for our security." At the same time, the President also stressed the urgency of his proposal, soon to be introduced into Congress as the Lend-Lease bill. "Emphatically we must get these weapons to them in sufficient volume and quickly enough, so that we and our children will be saved the agony and suffering of war which others have had to endure." Roosevelt's concluding words doubtless contributed to the unexpectedly enthusiastic response to the speech. "We must be the great arsenal of democracy," he declared. "For us this is an emergency as serious as war itself. We must apply ourselves to our task with the same resolution, the same sense of urgency, the same spirit of patriotism and sacrifice as we would show were we at war."[10]

"You have rallied America with a magnificent call," William Allen White immediately wired the President. "No patriot can withhold his support." Speaking for the Committee to Defend America by Aiding the Allies, he declared: "You have revived our faith in democracy here in our country and have made America again the light of the world. We proudly pledge you our full support." White's editorial the next day in the *Emporia Gazette* once more exploited parallels with the Civil War President. "Abraham Lincoln at Gettysburg did not more clearly and simply proclaim the cause men fought for eighty years ago than did President Roosevelt last night in his winged message that flew around the world. Americans have reason to be proud of the voice that spoke for them."[11]

5

If, in the public mind, William Allen White personified the Committee to Defend America by Aiding the Allies, its rival, America First, found in Charles Lindbergh a competing symbol. For millions of Americans he typified isolationism. The contrast between the images of the two men is instructive. White was a representative man, summing up in himself the attributes of a class and a region which, more than any others, had become identified with the genius of the nation. His own emergence had been gradual, paralleling that of the middle class and the Midwest for which he spoke. White represented the hero as apotheosis—in much the same sense as Lincoln.

Lindbergh, on the other hand, represented the hero as antithesis. While White reflected aspects of the national personality with which most Americans identified, the young aviator was a man set apart—somewhat in the manner of Robert E. Lee. His perennial youth, taciturnity, and diffidence contrasted squarely with the mellowed middle age, loquacity, and gregariousness of Will White. Unlike the editor, Lindbergh had emerged suddenly in 1927, on the strength of a single feat of skill and courage. The associations surrounding him were not social or regional but temporal. He became unalterably identified with the Twenties, even though—or perhaps because—in personality he contrasted with all the popular stereotypes. Far from exemplifying the American character, the handsome Lone Eagle, with his uncommon aeronautical aptitude, represented a new technological man, still somewhat of a stranger to Main Street. Not inappropriately, Lindbergh spent much of his life in seclusion or abroad. In all, because of its hybrid nature, his image was much more unstable than White's.

Briefly in 1941, Charles Lindbergh threatened to usurp the role of symbolic contemporary American in the continuing debate on foreign policy. Though he had delivered isolationist speeches since the outbreak of war in Europe, the Lone Eagle had avoided organizations supporting the same position. Finally, in April, 1941, he joined America First and immediately took a place on the executive committee. The leaders wasted no time pressing him into forensic service. They realized that, as a drawing card, the colonel had few peers. Within a week, Lindbergh delivered addresses at major rallies in Chicago and New York.

In his maiden speech for America First, at the Chicago Arena, Lindbergh insisted that all-out aid could not save Britain. But it would involve the United States in the war—a war the country could not win. "I believe that this war was lost by England and France even before it was declared," he asserted. Accordingly, "our real enemies," far from being the Axis aggressors, were the interventionists, whose "prime objective is to get us into the war."[12]

At his second appearance, six days later, Lindbergh drew an overflow crowd into Manhattan Center while many more listened in on the radio. Typically eschewing arguments of an idealistic nature, Lindbergh concentrated on the "practical" issues. "France has now been defeated," he declared, and ". . . England is losing the war." Whatever the interventionists might say, the United States could not alter the outcome. On both tactical and logistical grounds, he had "been forced to the conclusion that we cannot win this war for England, regardless of how much assistance we send."[13]

Supporters of aid to the Allies reacted with alarm. No one could deny Lindbergh's increasingly potent appeal. "He was undoubtedly Roosevelt's most formidable competitor on the radio," Robert Sherwood conceded afterward. Interventionists turned to the President for help. Why not silence the reserve colonel by recalling him to active duty? A reporter raised that very question at the next White House news conference, and Roosevelt, forewarned, skillfully played Lincoln to Lindbergh's Copperhead. "If you go back to the roster of the Army in the Civil War," the President reminded the press,

> —we called on . . . liberty-loving people on both sides . . . ; and from outside this country we had people fighting for us because they believed in it. On the other hand, the Confederacy and the North let people go. In other words, in both armies there were— what shall I call them?—there were Vallandighams.
>
> Well, Vallandigham, as you know, was an appeaser. He wanted to make peace from 1863 on because the North "couldn't win."

"Are you still talking about Colonel Lindbergh?" a reporter asked. According to *The New York Times*, the President gave a "simple and emphatic affirmative . . . answer." [14]

Hurt and angered by the comparison, Lindbergh publicly resigned his commission, explaining that he had "no honorable alternative" in view of Roosevelt's insinuations "concerning my loyalty." [15] In the following months, the aviator's speeches became more inflammatory, while interventionists, taking their cue from the President, increased the attack.

In June, at a national unity meeting in Chicago, Carl Sandburg condemned, with acid irony, the "famous flyer who has quit flying and taken to talking. . . ." While others had agonized over the fall of the European democracies, the poet declared, Lindbergh had remained impassive, "proud that he has ice instead of blood in his veins." "He calls interventionists like me hysterical," Sandburg exclaimed. "Very well, then we are hysterical. Very well, then the Declaration of Independence is hysterical, the Constitution of the United States is hysterical, the Bill of Rights is hysterical, the Gettysburg Speech and the Second Inaugural of Abraham Lincoln are hysterical—and the men who fought and died to establish those documents and give them meaning, they were all hysterical."[16]

In his newspaper columns of succeeding weeks, Sandburg filed additional indictments. Having identified himself with the great national tradition at Chicago, the poet sought to provide the "famous ex-flyer" with his own very different usable past. Lindbergh "holds theories of race discrimination and the color line quite the opposite of those held by Thomas Jefferson and Abraham Lincoln. . . ," he declared. Indeed, such ideas linked the isolationist with the infamous Know-Nothing Party of Lincoln's generation, one of whose slogans ran "Americans first!" The nativists and their works, he recalled, "gave Abraham Lincoln a troubled mind and a shaken soul," a reaction Lindbergh would doubtless label "hysteria." Nowhere in the utterances of "the one-time flyer" could Sandburg "find one hint of the passion for freedom and equality of opportunity that shook Lincoln. . . ."[17]

On September 14, Sandburg took Roosevelt's Civil War analogy even farther. "Lincoln would have liked to let this Congressman Vallandigham go on talking, because Vallandigham liked to hear himself talk and cloaked himself as a martyr," the poet wrote, emphasizing contemporary parallels. But the traitor's words might have undermined vital troop morale; and as Lincoln had once rhetorically asked: "Must I shoot a simple-minded soldier boy who deserts, while

I must not touch a hair of a wily agitator who induces him to desert?"[18]

Such attacks provoked more heated responses from Lindbergh. On September 11, 1941, in Des Moines, he blew the lid off the controversy by uttering the words which had so long been simmering under the surface of the isolationist campaign. The "three most important groups who have been pressing this country toward war," he declared, "are the British, the Jewish and the Roosevelt administration." Now all the suspicions of anti-Semitism, it seemed, were confirmed. But Lindbergh went on, inadvertently adding fuel to the flames with words which many took as a veiled threat. "Instead of agitating for war the Jewish groups in this country should be opposing it in every possible way, for they will be among the first to feel its consequences."[19] The speech brought an immediate and bitter response. All the pent-up frustrations that had been mounting since the outbreak of war two years before burst forth in a torrent of abuse upon the speaker. Charles Lindbergh, having made himself a spokesman for the Axis powers, now became the target for much of the antagonism they had generated in America. No wonder he suffered revilement out of proportion to the gravity of his words.

This time, as *The New York Times* noted, the President "remained aloof from the controversy." Like many others, however, his secretary, Steve Early, took note of the affinity of Lindbergh's statement with Nazi scapegoat tactics. He met reporters' questions with a series of propositions.

> You have seen the outpourings of Berlin in the last few days.
> You saw Lindbergh's statement last night.
> I think there is a striking similarity between the two.[20]

In one autumn evening, Charles Lindbergh ceased to be a national hero. William Allen White, symbol of an earlier and more enduring America, had the last word, expressing the sentiments of millions of Americans. "Shame on you, Charles

Lindbergh, for injecting the Nazi race issue into American politics," the editor wrote in his newspaper. "You can pillory the Jews if you will, or the Methodists or the Catholics if you dare, but alas in defending your inalienable right to speak your mind the Gazette cannot hold its silence at the moral treason of your words—at your unkind, unneighborly, dishonest words."[21]

For all its drama, the Lindbergh fiasco only confirmed what had already taken place. Americans had long since chosen their contemporary heroes, and the Lone Eagle did not belong among them. Through its shared possession by Roosevelt and White, however, the Lincoln image had become an inclusive vehicle for rallying Americans behind a nonpartisan interventionist foreign policy.

chapter seven

TWO POETS AND TWO PRESIDENTS

1

"He could have been Olympian, whimsical, seeking to be timeless amid bells of doom not to be put off," Carl Sandburg wrote in his dedication of *Home Front Memo*, a collection of his wartime propaganda pieces. But the poet whose memory he honored, Stephen Vincent Benét, "saw that a writer's silence on living issues can in itself constitute a propaganda of conduct leading toward the deterioration or death of freedom."[1] Sandburg's tribute might have applied as well to the author himself. During the year between the presidential election and Pearl Harbor, both men became unashamed propagandists. The two poets who had first heralded the resurgent Lincoln image now invoked the Great Emancipator's name in the defense of freedom and in the support of its defenders everywhere.

Stephen Vincent Benét's passion for the American past had sustained him in Paris during the Twenties. The onset of the Depression, shortly after he brought his family home, generated an interest in contemporary issues. Everywhere people talked politics, and the author of *John Brown's Body* joined in. His dynamic grounding in American history made him suspicious of radical panaceas, and also disdainful of reaction from the Right. Watching President Roosevelt weather attacks from both sides only reminded him of Lincoln's predicament and strengthened the liberalism which, as he said, kept one "always out on a limb." Benét's short stories of the period, drawing lightly veiled parallels between the past and the present, alarmed editors, who sought to blunt their bite. His poetry, too, revealed a growing social consciousness.

"These are your tan-faced children./ These skilled men, idle, with the holes in their shoes." In his "Ode to Walt Whitman," written in 1935, Benét addressed his spiritual ancestor, bringing out in a dialogue the mournful contrast between the promise of democracy foretold by the Civil War poet and its present frustration in the Depression. "Now they say we must have one tyranny or.another/ And a dark bell rings in our hearts." Hearing such sentiments, Benét's Whitman can only murmur: "Was the blood spilt for nothing, then?" The remainder of the poem, with its panoramic vision of America culminating in the mighty, lifegiving deity, the Mississippi, suggested not.[2] By 1935, Benét had found hope in the New Deal and its leadership.

Even more than domestic developments, the rise of totalitarianism abroad troubled the poet. Although in 1935 he had begun issuing his periodic poetic warnings—first, the stark "Litany for Dictatorships" and later some of the "Nightmares"—it took the Nazi blitzkrieg in the spring of 1940 to prepare the public for Benét's message. "Nightmare at Noon" appeared in *The New York Times Magazine* the day after the French surrender. Besides touching readers and later listeners who heard it dramatized on radio, the poem set a pattern of internal organization which Benét would continue to follow in succeeding public statements, whether in poetry or prose. Each contained a clear warning of danger, an appeal to American history, and then a call to action. Moreover, each patriotic utterance contained the same message: the rediscovered national past, no matter how heroic, could not supplant the need for a united reaffirmation of democratic principles in the contemporary crisis.

In "Nightmare at Noon," Benét had words of warning for complacent Americans who insisted that "There is time and time." Others had made the same miscalculation. "There was time in Norway and time, and the thing fell," he wrote. The people, "friendly and thriving and inventive" could not believe that war would come to their city. "When they woke, they saw the planes with the black crosses." Peaceful old Rotterdam, too, had fallen. "It was ended in a week, and the freedom ended." Now for America time was running out, he declared, acknowledging a national weakness. "We are slow to wake, good-natured as a country./ (It is our fault and our virtue.)" "We don't like war and we like to speak our minds," Benét stated. That might be part of the weakness. "There are certain words," the poet continued—words that had summed up the American achievement, words bought at great price. Twice he repeated the critical cadenced line from Lincoln's Emancipation Proclamation: "Thenceforward and forever free." But the once useful words had now become keepsakes; speeches would no longer suffice in lieu of action. "I am merely saying," Benét went on, "—what if these words pass?"[3]

Addressing the American Academy of Arts and Letters on "The Power of the Written Word," the poet stated his case in favor of propaganda. He called upon his fellow writers to join ranks with the greatest of their forebears who had confronted the crises and denounced the injustices of their own times. "We have seen, in the last few years," he continued, ". . . a tyranny set out to bind the minds of men for many ages." Contemporary dictators' very suppression of the literature of freedom bore witness to the power of words. "It remains for those of us who are free—and who mean to stay free—to consider what words we shall say and how we shall say them," Benét asserted. Writers, of course, could "call upon the great men, the great words of our own past—and that we should do—for in looking back at our past we can see at what price, by what endurance and fortitude, the freedom we have inherited was bought." But Americans must coin "new words also—and great ones—to match the present, to build for the future that must be."[4]

Despite an ingrained reticence, by the autumn of 1940, Benét had already taken his own exhortation to heart and enlisted in the battle of words. The postelection declaration of national unity, delivered by Raymond Massey, was only the most conspicuous of the speeches he produced that November. A week later, at historic Faneuil Hall in Boston, Theodore Morrison, the author, read another Benét summons. In "Democracy is the Revolution," the poet once again found a parallel in the national past. Like the Bostonians who had formed the first Committee of Correspondence 168 years before, Americans faced a threat to their freedom today. "And for that we arm in defense. But weapons alone will not defend the things we cherish," he declared. "We must defend them first in our hearts, in our minds, in our lives." Once more, in his prescription, Benét confronted the question of revitalizing words which had grown languid from continual usage on formal occasions. The truths of the eighteenth century remained valid, he emphasized, if only contemporary Americans would remember them. Paraphrasing the title of his speech, the poet concluded that "democracy . . . is the true revolution and has been from the first—the revolution against all those who would enslave man's body and mind. If we have forgotten that for a while, let us remember it now."[5]

Benét reached his largest audience—"more Americans than

any other serious writer in ... history," according to his biographer—on July 4, 1941, when NBC broadcast his poetic drama, "Listen to the People," in the time spot immediately preceding an address by President Roosevelt. Earlier in the week, *Life* magazine had published the script, urging its readers to listen to the program. Those who tuned in heard the most effective of all Benét's public statements. Afterward, the audience responded enthusiastically: telegrams and letters poured in to the poet, the periodical, and the network.[6]

This time Benét had married his characteristic tripartite organization with all the panoply of voices, music, and sound effects which radio afforded. Opening with the familiar voice of a narrator rattling off a catalogue of traditional Independence Day festivities, the script quickly interrupted the idyl with a chorus of discordant voices spouting the slogans of the class struggle, preaching hate and distrust, or ominously counseling capitulation. "Now be sensible—give up this corrupt and stupid nonsense of democracy." "Democracy is finished. We are the future."

Such voices meant death to Benét. "Are there no other voices?" The "long parade" of American history, to be sure, echoed with voices "never quite forgotten, always growing. ...." " 'I remember a man named Abe Lincoln./ I remember the words he used to say.'/ Oh, we can call on Lincoln and Tom Paine,/ Adams and Jefferson," according to the narrator.

> Call on the great words spoken that remain
> Like the great stars of evening, the fixed stars,
> But that is not enough.
> The dead are mighty and are a part of us
> And yet the dead are dead.
> This is our world,
> Our time, our choice, our anguish, our decision.

Even a revived American past, however firm a foundation, could not entirely compensate for a moribund past. Living

citizens must find their own voices—and so the poet listened
to a dissonant multitude, catalogued in the manner of Whitman's *Leaves of Grass*, speaking in the idiom of Sandburg's
The People, Yes.

> Our voice is not one voice but many voices.
> Not one man's, not the greatest, but the people's.
> The blue sky and the forty-eight States of the people.
> Many in easy times but one in the pinch
> And that's what some folks forget.

Then the awakened chorus of affirmation, one voice chiming
in after another until all unite in a pledge: "To liberty and
faith."

> What do the people say?
>   . . .
> We made this thing, this dream,
> This land unsatisfied by little ways,
> This peaceless vision, groping for the stars,
> Not as a huge devouring machine
> Rolling and clanking with remorseless force
> Over submitted bodies and the dead
> But as live earth where anything could grow,
> Your crankiness, my notions and his dream,
> Grow and be looked at, grow and live or die.
> But get their chance of growing and the sun.
> We made it and we make it and it's ours.
> We shall maintain it. It shall be sustained.[7]

"Listen to the People" marked both a climax and a beginning. While it capped the series of prophetic public
speeches—in prose and verse—that Benét had written to
awaken his countrymen to the dangers abroad, it also inaugurated his last brief but brilliant career as a radio dramatist. In
the months following Pearl Harbor, the poet turned out some
of the finest and most influential scripts of the war. Their
role in elevating morale earned praise from the government,
while their technical competence won the admiration of the
broadcast industry. But Benét's writing for the new medium,
no matter how eloquent, fell far short of his best in verse and

fiction. The scripts also interfered with the poet's other work, particularly his projected second verse epic. Its title borrowed from a poem addressed by Whitman to that other spokesman for America, Abraham Lincoln, *Western Star* remained a fragment at Benét's death in 1943. The frail poet had enlisted in the war effort and intended to serve for the duration, whatever the sacrifice.

2

Carl Sandburg too spoke out, both from the platform and in the press. While Benét sought to submerge his personality in his material, Sandburg gave to his own work a unique signature. No one else read *his* words from a rostrum: the tall, white-thatched troubadour voiced his own sentiments in his own twanging baritone. When his words appeared in print, as happened every week in his column for the *Chicago Times* syndicate, Sandburg's opinions carried his own byline. *The War Years* had made him a celebrity—a role he relished as much as the stooped, self-deprecating Benét would have detested it. Characteristically, the Chicago poet's pronouncements were more colloquial and candid than Benét's. Both in his support of aid to the Allies and in his attacks upon the isolationists, Sandburg expressed himself much more explicitly. In part, his choice of expository over poetic speech decreed this; but the purpose of his writing doubtless also influenced his decision to eschew verse.

The 1941 output from Sandburg's pen seemed all the more transient in contrast to *The War Years*. Writing columns and speeches on current topics, meeting ever-present deadlines, the poet produced uneven copy, more notable for compelling isolated phrases than overall conception. With the possible exception of a Lincoln piece for the Treasury Department, nothing he wrote distinguished even the profane genre of propaganda in the manner of Benét's better work. Sandburg, however, coveted his moral responsibility more than his aesthetic reputation, and spoke out.

Whether at a nationally broadcast rally or in his newspaper column, the poet continually invoked the name of Lincoln to support his own purposes. On the most encompassing level, the uses of the Great Emancipator were merely patriotic. Lincoln, the author of "a mystic, melancholy, involved definition of liberty"; and the embodiment of the people, "loving them with all their faults and failings." Lincoln, the spokesman for a "self-determining nation of politically free people"; and the champion of individualism, "respect for the human mind and the human personality. . . ." Audiences had come to expect Sandburg to make the familiar general references to the Great Emancipator. But Sandburg also marshaled the Lincoln lessons in behalf of specific causes. Increasingly he invoked the Great Emancipator's blessing upon the President. Assaying the "job of Chief Magistrate" on August 10, 1941, the poet concluded that Lincoln would have well understood the pressures on Franklin Roosevelt, and by implication, lauded his performance. A month later, in obliquely raising the question of the limits of freedom of speech in a period of national crisis, Sandburg reminded his readers how Lincoln had dealt with Clement Vallandigham, whose ⎽ame had become freighted with contemporary implications ever since Roosevelt linked it artfully with Charles Lindbergh's at his press conference of April 25. The poet devoted much of his November 30 column to the persistently urgent issue of national unity and once again concentrated on the lessons of Lincoln.[8]

Sandburg's most effective pairing of the two Presidents came in a widely circulated essay he wrote for the federal government. In President Roosevelt's cabinet, no man surpassed Henry Morgenthau, Jr. in devotion to his chief, faith in the American people, and commitment to the Allies.

Under him, the Treasury Department sponsored programs which reflected those enthusiasms. In 1941, Morgenthau commissioned twenty-eight distinguished American writers to "pay tribute" to an equal number of "giants in our past" in brief essays which were published in newspapers and later collected in a volume, *There Were Giants in the Land*. Of course, Carl Sandburg contributed the Lincoln portrait, the longest of the collection.

No author more effectively fulfilled his assignment to interpret his subject "in terms that would enlarge our understanding of the challenge we face today," as Morgenthau described it in his introduction. Sandburg made the parallels manifest. "What would Lincoln do now?" he asked, repeating a common contemporary question. Another query, "What did Lincoln do then?", provided the answer. What Lincoln did then, it seemed, was what Roosevelt was doing now.[9]

Looking back, one found timely solace in the conclusion that occasionally Lincoln too had been misunderstood; at times "what he did looked wrong to good men. . . ." As in his own time, Sandburg continued, if Lincoln were President today he would find himself continually caught in a crossfire of criticism. When he moved with dispatch to make great decisions he was called "tyrannical and despotic." When he refused or failed to so act, there were other epithets for him. Through it all, Lincoln kept his own counsel, responded to events as he thought appropriate, and confided to his astonished secretary, "My policy is to have no policy." Except, Sandburg added pointedly, "on the one issue of saving the Union and no extension of slavery, he had no fixed paramount policy."[10] Such manifestations of pragmatism sounded familiar to the generation of Franklin D. Roosevelt.

Gerald W. Johnson, reviewing the volume in the *New York Herald Tribune*, called Sandburg's contribution "superb," adding that "the parallel between Lincoln's troubles and those of a later war President is so close that it may be irritating to some people."[11] If so, they could blame the poet for calling it to their attention.

However artfully employed, though, the uses of Lincoln remained limited. Sandburg the public figure, whose celebrity emanated primarily from his identification with Lincoln, eventually felt compelled to dispense altogether with historical metaphor in enunciating his own position on aid to the Allies. With clarity at stake, the poet abandoned analogies. Still, the continuing association of the two figures in the public mind gave to Sandburg's words a special significance which, no doubt, helped account for his presence on public platforms. Besides, few speakers could match his ingenious identification with the folk. In a column in which he recalled his earlier vacillations on American policy, Sandburg confided that at times "I felt almost uncanny about the way my driftings were registered in the periodic shifts and gains and losses of the two leading polls of public opinion."[12]

He made a similar kind of claim at a crowded Unity Day meeting in the Chicago Stadium on June 7, 1941. "I have a suspicion," the poet declared, ". . . that my own drifting and shifting on the question whether we should throw all possible aid to Britain is somewhat the same story of exactly the same kind of drifting and shifting that has taken place in the minds and hearts of millions of Americans." Sandburg then traced his own evolution into an interventionist, a story familiar to readers of one of his earlier columns. The Nazi victories of the previous spring had triggered the change. "When the Republic of France was crushed in dust and shame I was one of the millions of Americans who saw that Britain was next on the Nazi timetable," he recalled. Determined that lack of materiel should never bring Britain down, Sandburg had become "an insignificant unit among the millions whose talk and feeling made possible the decisive vote in Congress by which the Lend-Lease Bill was passed."[13]

Now, even lend-lease seemed insufficient. Reluctantly the

poet conceded that "unless we see to it that the help we want to give Britain reaches her shores, we are taking the risk of her going down, and if she goes down we will have had a hand in it by our neglect and hesitation." Nazi threats could not dismay the speaker. "I am one of the millions in this country," he announced, "who believe that if we now let Hitler tell us we can't do this or we can't do that, we will later either again let him tell us what we can or can't do—or in that later time we will take the only course open to us, that of fighting a long and bloody war." Beyond that, Sandburg refused to go. Altogether, he concluded, "I am taking my chances with those who say 'God bless the President of the United States,' "[14] a phrase he repeated at the end of an August speech to a similar nationally broadcast rally in Madison Square Garden.

Sandburg's weekly newspaper columns charted his movement toward unlimited interventionism. Perhaps it was all inevitable: in looking back, he confessed that the destroyers-for-bases deal of the previous year had come "so near to a declaration of war . . . that the point was merely technical." Regardless, the poet found himself approving "the war of nerves" the President was waging against the Nazis, a sentiment he reiterated in an August column in which he catalogued the various executive moves, concluding that

> Through our President we seem to Europe as a whole people and a united people to be standing up and saying we are going to throw in everything we have to smash Hitler. Does this bother and annoy the Nazis? It does. They want the suspense over. They like to calculate. And we are the incalculable.

So was the future. Even in the autumn Sandburg would hazard no more than that "time will tell us . . . whether this country will have to fight a war—a long, heavy, bloody war—against the whole outside world."[15] When the time came, the government could thank Carl Sandburg and Stephen Vincent Benét for helping alert the public to the need to prepare for action.

3

Franklin Roosevelt, who had often quoted Abraham Lincoln for his own political purposes, now sought to exploit parallels with the Great Emancipator to provide historical justification for his nonpartisan foreign policy. On two occasions, he explicitly associated his own situation with that of the Civil War Commander-in-Chief.

The first was a customarily partisan event. In the post-inauguration climate of national unity, however, it seemed inappropriate for the President to deliver a conventional message to the traditional Jackson Day dinners across the nation. Accordingly, he instructed his writers, Samuel Rosenman and Robert Sherwood, to draft a nonpartisan speech. Roosevelt's address, broadcast from the yacht *Potomac* in Florida, went out to all Americans; and his use of the past knew no party boundaries. In a Nazi-dominated world, he reminded his listeners, there would be neither a Jackson Day nor a Lincoln Day.[16]

Indeed, Roosevelt's closing words seemed more appropriate to the latter occasion. Spanning the four score years that separated them, he drew a timely comparison between his own predicament and the secession crisis that had confronted the first Republican Chief Executive. "When Abraham Lincoln became President, he had to face the awful reality of a war between the States," Roosevelt declared.

> On July 4, 1861, in his first message to Congress, he presented this vital question:
> "Must a government, of necessity, be too strong for the liberties of its own people, or too weak to maintain its own existence?"
> Lincoln answered that question as Jackson had answered it— not by words, but by deeds. And America still marches on.

We of today have been presented with that same question. We too are answering it by deeds. Our well-considered philosophy for the attainment of peace comes not from weakness but—everlastingly—from the courage of America.[17]

The second occasion, in August 1941, was the President's first press conference after his Atlantic Conference with Winston Churchill. As expected, the questions turned to the British assessment of the war. One reporter inquired if the Prime Minister "seemed confident" that Britain could win the war without American military intervention. Though hesitant to quote Churchill for the record, Roosevelt could still indicate that long-range optimism reigned at 10 Downing Street. Then, using the question as a pretext, the President proceeded to make a related point. What concerned both leaders, he explained, was the tendency, all too evident in democracies, to become complacent in the face of such assurances. "And of course," Roosevelt continued, "that can't be justified. . . . On the contrary, when you're winning, or when things look a little bit better, that's the time for you to redouble your efforts."[18]

Then, shuffling through the papers in his workbasket, Roosevelt came up with a telling illustration recently "dug out" of Carl Sandburg's *The War Years*. The President read the reporters a passage dealing with Lincoln's remarks to a delegation of ladies who waited upon him at the end of the first year of the Civil War, seeking some comforting statement on the outcome of the conflict. Lincoln regretted that he had "no word of encouragement to give"; but, he sighed, "the people have not yet made up their minds that we are at war with the South."

"That is rather an interesting parallel," the President observed when he had finished reading from the biography. "Lincoln's belief that this country hadn't yet waked up to the fact, that they had a war to win, and Lincoln saw what had been going on. Well, there are quite a lot of things for us to think about in this day and age."

One impertinent reporter piped up, "Mr. President, if you were going to write a lead on that, how would you do it?"

Roosevelt welcomed the opportunity to drive home the point by composing his own headline. "I'd say," he replied, " 'President Quotes Lincoln—And Draws Parallel.' "[19]

Judging from *The New York Times*, journalists approved the work of the copy editor in the White House. Next day on page one, the *Times'* headline ran: "President Bids Nation Awake to Peril/ Roosevelt is Grim/ Quotes Lincoln to Show a Parallel Between Those Days and These." Moreover, in its lead editorial on the following day, the newspaper agreed that the "significance" of the parallel Roosevelt drew would "not be lost on anybody."[20]

4

As the year came to an end and the nation mobilized for war, *Time* magazine announced its "Man of the Year." To no one's surprise, it was Franklin D. Roosevelt. In discussing their choice, however, the editors of the weekly news magazine displayed a rare appreciation of the President's historical role. "The U.S. has had five war Presidents in its history, and for Lincoln, the greatest of them, the war was civil war," they wrote. "In the wars with foreign foes, Madison, Polk, McKinley, Wilson—predecessors of President Roosevelt—faced no such task as he faces." No matter how unprecedented the challenge, however, the President had already demonstrated his ability to inspire and lead the nation, as *Time* acknowledged. In 1933 Americans who had been "beaten by the hopelessness of the Depression were electrified" by Roosevelt's words and actions.

> But the hopelessness they had felt then was nothing compared to the hopelessness that was felt by millions over the world in 1941.

The relief and release that U.S. citizens felt in 1933, when the President broke the paralysis that had gripped them, was nothing compared to the lifting of heads all over the world when the power and might of the U.S. was thrown into the war. Once he had told the people of the U.S.: "This generation has a rendezvous with destiny." Now there could be no mistaking the fact. He was the man of 1941 because the country he leads stands for the hope of the world.[21]

Even in the words of an unfriendly press, Franklin Roosevelt had by 1942 assumed heroic symbolic proportions.

chapter eight

CONCLUSION

1

By the time of his death, only weeks before the end of the Second World War, Franklin D. Roosevelt had achieved a popular stature equal to that of Abraham Lincoln. Indeed, in public opinion polls of 1945 and 1946, he ranked even higher than the Great Emancipator. Another canvass, ten years later, confirmed that Roosevelt's public esteem represented much more than a temporary reaction to his passing.[1] Death on the threshold of victory served the President in other ways, however. As with Lincoln, it removed him from the scene almost at the moment of his triumph—before postwar controversies could tarnish his glory. But this represented only the last of many parallels between the two wartime chief executives.

With "firmness in the right, as God gives us to see the right, let us strive to finish the work we are in. . . ." The words were Lincoln's, the President told the 1944 Democratic national convention, but they were "as applicable today as they were in 1865. . . ." Presidential campaigns always provide an opportunity for historical comparisons, and once again Franklin Roosevelt gladly took advantage of the situation. Stumping late in October, he pointedly reminded an audience that "we are holding a national election while the Nation is at war" for the first time since 1864, and then quoted Lincoln at the expense of contemporary Republicans. Nothing Roosevelt said, however, could compare with the analogy provided by the war itself. Although the President had been linked with Abraham Lincoln long before Pearl Harbor, it was as Commanders-in-Chief that their careers finally converged. Each unified the nation behind a war which he defined in moral terms. Each inspired his followers with eloquent appeals to self-sacrifice. Each prosecuted the struggle to a successful conclusion. And, of course, each died in April, on the eve of final victory, as Eleanor Roosevelt pointed out in a newspaper column a few days after her husband's death.[2]

Aside from the patent historical parallels, however, what special qualities of Lincoln had attracted Roosevelt and the writers who contributed to the comparison? For them, appropriately, Lincoln symbolized nothing new or novel. He still stood for the democratic conviction that an unfettered people could overcome any challenge. He still represented a commitment to human freedom—embodied in the Emancipation Proclamation—and to social democracy—symbolized by his own rise from the humblest of origins. These old precepts were not altered but revitalized by the authors who wrote so affectionately about Abe Lincoln. By recreating his youth on the prairies—in a poetic biography and a dramatic chronicle—Sandburg and Sherwood attempted to make the Great Emancipator more approachable. In their epic works on his Presidency, Benét and Sandburg raised this humanized Lincoln even higher. But the man they honored was essentially the same one whose star had been rising ever since the Civil War.

Lincoln's high place in American history stemmed from a combination of personal qualities and historic circumstances.

His rise from frontier obscurity to the White House contained drama enough to inspire a host of storytellers. Aspects of his character—the homely wit, gentle tolerance of human nature, unaffected wisdom and understanding—seemed preternaturally "American." The heroic tasks Lincoln accomplished as Civil War President, of course, contributed profoundly to his standing. Finally, the principles he embodied and enunciated won him an honored place among the prophets of freedom and democracy.

No matter how different, Franklin Roosevelt's first fifty years also bore intimations of greatness. His name tied him closely to one famous President and his government service linked him with another. His own record as a reforming New York state senator established his reputation as an independent liberal. Perhaps even more important for his later popular image, Roosevelt's battle with poliomyelitis during the Twenties not only demonstrated his courage and determination but also constituted, in a sense, his rite of passage. Almost a decade before the Great Crash, he learned the lessons of suffering and developed the humility, compassion, and serene self-confidence which inspired his countrymen during his years in the White House. The Great Depression and the Second World War, of course, presented Roosevelt with an almost unparalleled opportunity to fulfill his heroic potential. But equally important, he seized the time— inspiring confidence with his reassuring words and bold leadership—and the nation rallied behind him. In Roosevelt's case, too, character and circumstance converged to mold presidential greatness. But historic parallels with Lincoln provided an additional dimension to Roosevelt's image and accomplishments. And for that he could thank the writers who had revitalized Lincoln's memory and pointed to his example in their own time.

2

Even before the election of 1944, two of the individuals who had contributed notably to the political uses of the Lincoln image had died. While their strength remained, however, William Allen White and Stephen Vincent Benét had contributed in their own fashion to the national war effort.

Pearl Harbor signaled no end to the Emporia editor's battle against isolationism. The America First mentality could still pervert national purposes, White argued, if it reemerged after the Allied victory. Middle Westerners especially must "understand that only as the United States takes leadership in some kind of a world association, union, alliance or treaty-making organization to promote economic justice on a world scale will we be able to reduce the likelihood of war." Crucial to the realization of any such role, of course, was a reinvigorated Republican Party, ready with positive alternatives to the Democratic programs. "If only the Republican party that gave us Lincoln would forget its hatred of Roosevelt, get rid of its bias toward plutocracy, get back to the grass roots and the hearts of the people . . ," he declared in a now familiar vein.[3] William Allen White continued to agitate for those dual objectives until he succumbed of a heart attack on January 29, 1944.

For Stephen Vincent Benét, a new impulse—to interpret the American experience to an international audience—accompanied the declaration of war. In 1942, the Office of War Information commissioned the poet to write a short, impressionistic history of the United States for overseas propaganda purposes. In *America*, published in 1944, he created a simple, informal prose poem suitable for ready translation into every modern language. Only Benét's untimely death prevented him from witnessing the widespread distribution of the book.

At the center of his national portrait Benét sketched the

familiar figure of Abraham Lincoln for the world to see. From his humble origins, the folk Lincoln emerged again, in the proverbial words and deeds. Before he began to recount the American story, Benét had asked: "What is the American spirit, the American idea?" The Lincoln chapter provided the answers. In the words of the Gettysburg Address and the Second Inaugural, the poet insisted, "there breathes the American spirit, and it was in that spirit that Abraham Lincoln made war. And had he been permitted to make peace, he would have made it in that spirit."[4]

At the close of his narrative, when he brought the account to the present—which had never been lost in his version of the past—Benét confronted the Fascist enemies with a declaration of national determination climaxed by the echo of Lincoln's "House Divided" speech which had served William Allen White so well: "we will fight this war till the governments of the Axis countries are crushed to the earth, their dictatorships abolished from the memory of man. . . . For, as we could not live in a country half free, so we cannot live in a world half free and half slave."[5]

Interpreting American purposes to a world at war also occupied Robert E. Sherwood. His affiliation with the Roosevelt Administration entered a new phase during the last days of 1941. Even before Pearl Harbor, the playwright undertook to organize overseas propaganda programs for the government. First under the auspices of the Coordinator of Information and then as part of Elmer Davis' Office of War Information, Sherwood supervised the development of a far-flung network of propaganda operations. Not even the exigencies of war, however, could goad the author of *Abe Lincoln in Illinois* into deliberate distortion of the truth. In his mind, the American cause needed no embellishments; accordingly, the Overseas Branch of the OWI devoted its programs primarily to factual news reports.

As if to complement Sherwood's endeavors, Carl Sandburg

directed his attention to the home front audience. In the continuing series of his syndicated weekly newspaper columns, the Chicago poet honored the unsung heroes of the war, at home and abroad, American and Allied, as befitted the renowned spokesman for the common man. Analogies between the present and the past sprang readily to the Lincoln biographer's mind. His columns abounded with references to suggestive parallels with the Civil War era.

When *Home Front Memo*, a collection of Sandburg's wartime writings, was published in 1943, it met a respectful reception from the reviewers. None, however, quite approached the *Chicago Sun's* August Derleth in attributing a Lincolnian character to the author. "Over the entire book hovers the spirit of Lincoln," he declared.

> Indeed, Sandburg has for so long been saturated in Lincoln lore that even his thought-pattern is Lincoln's. . . . Sandburg is preoccupied with Lincoln almost to the extent of being haunted by him. Not only does the book lead off with five Lincoln pieces, drawing a strong parallel between the Civil War President in his years of travail, and Roosevelt today, but Lincoln constantly recurs in the book as a kind of theme with variations.[6]

Lincoln, Roosevelt, Sandburg—by 1943 the collaboration was complete.

The emergence of a revitalized Lincoln image in the era of the New Deal and the Second World War testified to the influence of three liberal middlebrow writers—two poets and a playwright—who helped fortify a President and a people for the crucial tasks they faced. The memory of Abraham Lincoln had never failed the nation; but the capacity to recall the lessons of the Great Emancipator during the era of Franklin D. Roosevelt owed much to Carl Sandburg, Stephen Vincent Benét, and Robert E. Sherwood.

BIBLIOGRAPHICAL NOTE

In exploring the political uses of the revitalized Lincoln image of Sandburg, Benét, and Sherwood, the author has drawn upon selected materials from a variety of sources, as indicated in the preceding chapters. Because of the subjective nature of the topic, no formal bibliography has been appended. Instead, some of the more important areas of investigation are indicated below.

The revival of interest in the American past that accompanied the Depression is recounted in a number of sources, notably Alfred Kazin, *On Native Grounds* (New York: Reynal & Hitchcock, 1942) and Henry Steele Commager, *The American Mind* (New Haven: Yale University Press, 1950). No comprehensive study of the phenomenon, however, has yet appeared.

Biographical information on the principal figures in this study is available in numerous sources of varying worth. The Roosevelt literature, of course, is vast and uneven. Of works on the writers, the most valuable are Walter Johnson, *William Allen White's America* (New York: Henry Holt and Company, 1947) and Charles A. Fenton, *Stephen Vincent Benét: The Life and Times· of an American Man of Letters,*

1898-1943 (New Haven: Yale University Press, 1958). The concluding volume of John Mason Brown's definitive life of Sherwood, *The Ordeal of a Playwright: Robert E. Sherwood and the Challenge of War* (New York: Harper & Row, Publishers, 1970), remained unfinished at the author's death. The first, *The Worlds of Robert E. Sherwood: Mirror to His Times* (New York: Harper & Row, Publishers, 1965), takes its subject up to 1939. North Callahan, *Carl Sandburg: Lincoln of Our Literature* (New York: New York University Press, 1970), the latest biography, like its predecessors, is based on printed sources. Published speeches of the President, as well as writings of the two poets and the playwright, the veritable foundation of this study, are extensively paraphrased and quoted throughout.

Given the character of this study, manuscript collections have only limited uses. The author has consulted those deemed pertinent. The Franklin D. Roosevelt papers at Hyde Park and the William Allen White papers at the Library of Congress have proved valuable in revealing informal intercourse among some of the principals. Neither the Carl Sandburg nor the Robert E. Sherwood papers is now open to the public. The Stephen Vincent Benét papers at the Yale University Library have been of little value to the purposes of this study.

Collections of the Sandburg, White, and Benét correspondence have been published: Herbert Mitgang (ed.), *The Letters of Carl Sandburg* (New York: Harcourt Brace Jovanovich, Inc., 1968); Walter Johnson (ed.), *Selected Letters of William Allen White, 1899-1943* (New York: Henry Holt and Company, 1947); and Charles A. Fenton (ed.), *Selected Letters of Stephen Vincent Benét* (New Haven: Yale University Press, 1960).

The study of American myths and symbols, first suggested by Ralph Henry Gabriel, and brilliantly undertaken in Henry Nash Smith's *Virgin Land: The American West as Symbol and Myth* (Cambridge: Harvard University Press, 1950), has brought valuable results in at least two other instances. John William Ward, in *Andrew Jackson: Symbol for an Age* (New York: Oxford University Press, 1955), has imaginatively examined Old Hickory's impact upon his own generation, while Merrill D. Peterson's *The Jefferson Image in the American Mind* (New York: Oxford University Press, 1960) exhaustively traces the changing interpretations of the Sage of Monticello since his own time.

No comparable studies of the Lincoln image exist, although a handful of works treat aspects of the subject. Closest to a full-scale interpretation is Roy P. Basler, *The Lincoln Legend: A Study of Changing Conceptions* (Boston: Houghton Mifflin Company, 1935). Michael Davis, *The Image of Lincoln in the South* (Knoxville: University of Tennessee Press, 1971), is limited to the nineteenth century. Brief but suggestive discussions of the Lincoln image can be found in Ralph Henry Gabriel, *The Course of American Democratic Thought* (New York: The Ronald Press Company, 1940); Dixon Wecter, *The Hero in America: A Chronicle of Hero-Worship* (New York: Charles Scribner's Sons, 1941); Marshall W. Fishwick, *American Heroes: Myth and Reality* (Washington, D.C.: Public Affairs Press, 1954); John Morton Blum, *The Promise of America: An Historical Inquiry* (Boston: Houghton Mifflin Company, 1966); and David Donald, *Lincoln Reconsidered: Essays on the Civil War Era* (New York: Alfred A. Knopf, 1956). The first chapter of the last work helped inspire this study.

NOTES

notes to chapter 1

1. Alfred Kazin, *On Native Grounds: An Interpretation of Modern American Prose Literature* (New York: Reynal and Hitchcock, 1942), p. 487; Merle Curti, *The Growth of American Thought* (New York: Harper & Brothers, 1951), p. 740; Harold Clurman, *The Fervent Years: The Story of the Group Theatre and the Thirties* (New York: Alfred A. Knopf, 1945), p. 20.

2. Van Wyck Brooks, "On Creating a Usable Past," *The Dial*, LXIV (April 11, 1918), 339.

3. Van Wyck Brooks, *America's Coming-of-Age* (New York: B. W. Huebsch, 1915), p. 121; "On Creating a Usable Past," *Dial*, April 11, 1918, pp. 340, 341.

4. Waldo Frank, *The Re-discovery of America: An Introduction to a Philosophy of American Life* (New York: Charles Scribner's Sons, 1929), p. 318.

5. *The Seven Arts*, I (November 1916), 52; II (October 1917), v.

6. Frederick J. Hoffman, *The Twenties: American Writing in the Postwar Decade* (New York: The Viking Press, 1955), p. 122.

7. Stephen Vincent Benét, "A Defense of Mrs. Anonymous," *The Bookman*, LXIV (October 1926), 169; Claude M. Fuess, "Debunkery and Biography," *The Atlantic Monthly*, CLI (March 1933), 347; Bernard DeVoto, "The Skeptical Biographer," *Harper's Magazine*, CLXVI (January 1933), 190.

8. John Dos Passos, *The Ground We Stand On: Some Examples from the History of a Political Creed* (New York: Harcourt Brace Jovanovich, Inc., 1941), p. 3.

9. Quoted in Bernard Smith, "The Liberals Grow Old," *The Saturday Review of Literature*, X (December 30, 1933), 378.

10. Dos Passos, *The Ground We Stand On*, p. 3.

11. Louis Bromfield, "Expatriate—Vintage 1927," *The Saturday Review of Literature*, III (March 19, 1927), 1; Harold Stearns, *Rediscovering America* (New York: Horace Liveright, 1934), p. 135; Malcolm Cowley, *Exile's Return: A Literary Odyssey of the 1920s* (New York: The Viking Press, 1951), pp. 11-12.

12. Allen Johnson (ed.), *Dictionary of American Biography*, I (New York: Charles Scribner's Sons, 1928), viii.

13. William E. Lingelbach (ed.), *Approaches to American Social History* (New York: D. Appleton-Century Co., 1937), p. 84.

14. Malcolm Cowley, "The 1930's Were an Age of Faith," *The New York Times Book Review*, December 13, 1964, p. 14.

15. Alfred Kazin, "What Have the 30's Done to Our Literature?," *New York Herald Tribune Books*, December 31, 1939, p. 1.

16. Carl Becker, *New York Herald Tribune Books*, October 9, 1938, p. 2.

17. Allan Nevins, "What's the Matter with History?," *The Saturday Review of Literature*, XIX (February 4, 1939), 3; Edgar Johnson, "American Biography and the Modern World," *The North American Review*, CCXLV (Summer 1938), 368, 379.

18. Alfred Kazin, *New York Herald Tribune Books*, December 31, 1939, p. 1.

notes to chapter 2

1. Basil Rauch (ed.), *The Roosevelt Reader* (New York: Holt, Rinehart and Winston, 1957), p. 44.

2. *Ibid.*, pp. 45, 47.

3. Irving Brant, *Storm Over the Constitution* (Indianapolis: The Bobbs-Merrill Co., 1936), p. 40.

4. *The New York Times*, January 26, 1936, p. 36.

5. Carl Sandburg, *Abraham Lincoln: The Prairie Years* (New York: Harcourt Brace Jovanovich, Inc., 1926), II, 233.

6. Carl Sandburg, *The Complete Poems of Carl Sandburg* (New York: Harcourt Brace Jovanovich, 1916), p. 172.

7. Stuart Sherman, "Carl Sandburg's Lincoln," *New York Herald Tribune Books,* February 7, 1926, p. 2.

8. Sandburg, *The Prairie Years*, I, vii.

9. *Ibid.*, I, 177.

10. Henry Seidel Canby, "Stephen Vincent Benét," *The Saturday Review of Literature*, XXVI (March 27, 1943), 14.

11. Henry Seidel Canby, " 'His Soul Goes Marching On,' " *The Saturday Review of Literature*, V (September 29, 1928), 163.

12. Stephen Vincent Benét, *John Brown's Body* (New York: Rinehart & Company, Inc., 1928), pp. 61, 98, 179, 196.

13. Roy P. Basler, *The Lincoln Legend: A Study in Changing Conceptions* (Boston: Houghton Mifflin Co., 1935), p. 295.

14. *Ibid.* p. 226.

15. *Federal Theatre Plays* (New York: Random House, 1938), p. 7.

16. Brooks Atkinson, "Lincoln of New Salem," *The New York Times*, March 27, 1938, X, 1.

17. *The New York Times*, August 26, 1938, p. 19; Hallie Flanagan, *Arena* (New York: Duell, Sloan and Pearce, 1940), p. 173.

18. *Federal Theatre Plays*, x-xi.

notes to chapter 3

1. Joseph Mersand, *The Play's the Thing: Enjoying the Plays of Today* (New York: The Modern Chapbooks, 1941), p. 75; Maxwell Anderson, "Robert E. Sherwood," *Theatre Arts*, XL (February 1956), 87; Brooks Atkinson, *The New York Times*, October 23, 1938, IX, 1.

2. Robert Emmet Sherwood, *Abe Lincoln in Illinois* (New York: Charles Scribner's Sons, 1939), p. 191.

3. Euphemia Van Rensselaer Wyatt, *The Catholic World*, CXLVIII (December, 1938), 340.

4. Sherwood, *Abe Lincoln in Illinois*, pp. 189, 190.

5. *Ibid.*, pp. 190-191.

6. Elmer Rice, *Minority Report: An Autobiography* (New York: Simon and Schuster, 1963), p. 382.

7. Robert E. Sherwood to Franklin D. Roosevelt, April 20, 1939. Franklin D. Roosevelt Papers, OF 80. Hyde Park.

8. Harold Clurman, *The Nation*, CXCVI (February 9, 1963), 125; Frank H. O'Hara, *Today in America Drama* (Chicago: University of Chicago Press, 1939), pp. 103; *The New York Times*, October 30, 1938, IX, 3.

9. *The New York Times*, December 11, 1938, X, 5.

10. Sherwood, *Abe Lincoln in Illinois*, pp. 137, 153.

11. *Ibid.*, pp. 233, 137-138.

12. *Ibid.*, p. 138.

13. Robert E. Sherwood to Franklin D. Roosevelt, January 25, 1940. Roosevelt Papers, PPF 1820; *The Saturday Review of Literature*, XIX (February 18, 1939), 7.

14. Robert E. Sherwood, *There Shall Be No Night* (New York: Charles Scribner's Sons, 1940), p. xxiii.

15. *The New York Times*, October 30, 1938, IX, 3; Sherwood, *There Shall Be No Night*, p.xxv.

16. Sherwood, *There Shall Be No Night*, p. xxiv; *Abe Lincoln in Illinois*, pp. 139-140.

17. Sherwood, *Abe Lincoln in Illinois*, p. 183.

18. Robert E. Sherwood, *The New York Times*, February 25, 1940, IX, 4; John Mosher, *The New Yorker*, February 24, 1940, p. 67.

19. Philip T. Hartung, *The Commonweal*, XXXI (February 16, 1940), 367; *Life*, VIII (February 12, 1940), 76-77; Presidential Press Conference No. 617 (January 23, 1940), Roosevelt Papers. Vol. 15: 95.

20. Bernard DeVoto, "The Easy Chair," *Harper's Magazine*, CLXXX (February 1940), 333.

notes to chapter 4

1. Harry Golden, *Carl Sandburg* (Cleveland: The World Publishing Company, 1961), p. 240; Carl Sandburg, *A Lincoln Preface* (New York: Harcourt Brace Jovanovich, Inc., 1953), n.p.; Carl Detzer, *Carl Sandburg: A Study in Personality and Background* (New York: Harcourt Brace Jovanovich, Inc., 1941), p. 175.

2. Richard Crowder, *Carl Sandburg* (New York: Twayne Publishers, Inc., 1964), pp. 124-125.

3. Carl Sandburg, *The People, Yes* (New York: Harcourt Brace Jovanovich, Inc., 1936), p. 134.

4. Benjamin P. Thomas, *Portrait for Posterity: Lincoln and His Biographers* (New Brunswick, N.J.: Rutgers University Press, 1947), p. 296; *The Lincoln of Carl Sandburg* (New York: Harcourt, Brace and Company, n.d.).

5. James G. Randall, *The American Historical Review*, XLV (July 1940), 918; Stephen Vincent Benét, *The Atlantic Monthly*, CLXIV (December 1939), n.p.; Charles A. Beard, *The Virginia Quarterly Review*, XVI (Winter 1940), 112; Lloyd Lewis, *New York Herald Tribune Books*, December 3, 1939, IX, 3; Allan Nevins, *The Saturday Review of Literature*, XXI (December 2, 1939), 4; Henry Bertram Hill, *Kansas City Star*, December 2, 1939, reprinted in *Lincoln of Carl Sandburg*, p. 37.

6. Lewis, *Books*, December 3, 1939, IX, 3; Henry Steele Commager, *The Yale Review*, XXIX (Winter 1940), 374; Max Lerner, *The New Republic*, CI (December 6, 1939), 197; Nevins, *Saturday Review*, December 2, 1939, p. 3; Randall, *American Historical Review*, July 1940, pp. 917-918.

7. Robert E. Sherwood, *The New York Times Book Review*, December 3, 1939, p. 1.

8. Commager, *Yale Review*, Winter 1940, p. 375; Beard, *Virginia*

Review, Winter 1940, p. 113; Nevins, *Saturday Review*, December 2, 1939, p. 20.

9. Carl Sandburg, *Abraham Lincoln: The War Years* (New York: Harcourt Brace Jovanovich, Inc., 1939), II, 333.

10. Sandburg, *The War Years*, II, 332-333.

11. *Ibid.*, III, 383.

12. *Ibid.*, III, 559.

13. *Ibid.*, II, 275.

14. *Ibid.*, II, 275; Carl Sandburg, *A Lincoln and Whitman Miscellany* (Chicago: Holiday Press, 1938), p. 29.

15. Sandburg, *The War Years*, II, 277; IV, 385.

16. *Ibid.*, IV, 297.

17. *Ibid.*, IV, 377.

18. *Ibid.*, IV, 385.

19. Sherwood, *The New York Times*, December 3, 1939, p. 1.

20. Sandburg, *The War Years*, III, 567; IV, 387.

21. Commager, *Yale Review*, Winter 1940, p. 29; Nevins, *Saturday Review*, December 2, 1939, p. 22; Lerner, *New Republic*, December 6, 1939, p. 197.

22. Benét, *The Atlantic Monthly*, December, 1939, n.p.

23. Carl Sandburg, *Storm Over the Land: A Profile of the Civil War* (New York: Harcourt Brace Jovanovich, Inc., 1942), n.p.

notes to chapter 5

1. Ralph Henry Gabriel, *The Course of American Democratic Thought* (New York: The Ronald Press Company, 1940), pp. 396, 397, 409.

2. Dixon Wecter, *The Hero in America: A Chronicle of Hero-Worship* (New York: Charles Scribner's Sons, 1941), pp. 460-461.

3. *Public Papers and Addresses of Franklin D. Roosevelt. 1938 Volume: The Continuing Struggle for Liberalism* (New York: The Macmillan Company, 1941), p. 520.

4. Donald Day, *Franklin D. Roosevelt's Own Story* (Boston: Little, Brown & Co., 1951), p. 120.

5. *The Public Papers and Addresses of Franklin D. Roosevelt. Vol. Three: The Advance of Recovery and Reform, 1934* (New York: Random House, 1938), p. 422.

6. *The Public Papers and Addresses of Franklin D. Roosevelt. Volume Five: The People Approve, 1936* (New York: Random House, 1938), p. 222; *The Public Papers and Addresses of Franklin D. Roosevelt. 1937 Volume: The Constitution Prevails* (New York: The Macmillan Co., 1941), p. 129.

7. *The Public Papers and Addresses of Franklin D. Roosevelt. 1938 Volume*, pp. 37-42.

8. *Public Papers and Addresses of Franklin D. Roosevelt. 1938 Volume*, pp. 419-421.

9. Emil Ludwig, *Roosevelt: A Study in Fortune and Power* (New York: The Viking Press, 1938), p. 341; Carl Sandburg to Franklin D. Roosevelt, March 9, 1938. Franklin D. Roosevelt Papers, PPF4509. Hyde Park; Max Lerner, "Roosevelt and History," *The Nation*, CXLVI (May 7, 1938), 534; Raymond Moley, "The Class of 1939," *Newsweek*, XIII (June 19, 1939), 56; Richard L. Neuberger, "Some Like Roosevelt," *The Nation*, CXLVII (July 2, 1938), 7.

10. *The New York Times*, February 14, 1939, p. 14.

11. *Congressional Record*, February 12, 1936, p. 1940.

12. *Public Papers and Addresses of Franklin D. Roosevelt. 1938 Volume*, p. 38; *The Public Papers and Addresses of Franklin D. Roosevelt. 1939 Volume: War–and Neutrality* (New York: The Macmillan Company, 1941), p. 65; *The Public Papers and Addresses of Franklin D. Roosevelt. 1940 Volume: War–and Aid to the Democracies* (New York: The Macmillan Company, 1941), p. 30.

13. *The New York Times*, February 13, 1940, p. 25.

14. James MacGregor Burns, *Roosevelt: The Lion and the Fox* (New York: Harcourt, Brace and Company, 1956), p. 423.

15. Max Lerner, "The Lincoln Image," *The New Republic*, XCVIII (March 8, 1939), 135; "Men Who Would Be President: IX. Franklin D. Roosevelt," *The Nation*, CI (June 22, 1940), 753-754.

16. John Mason Brown, *The Worlds of Robert E. Sherwood: Mirror to His Times, 1896-1939* (New York: Harper & Row, Publishers, 1965), p. 385; Robert E. Sherwood to Franklin D. Roosevelt, January 25, 1940. Roosevelt Papers, PPF 1820.

17. Samuel I. Rosenman, *Working with Roosevelt* (New York: Harper & Brothers, 1952), p. 228; Robert E. Sherwood, *Roosevelt and Hopkins: An Intimate History* (New York: Harper & Brothers, 1948), p. 184.

18. Rosenman, *Working with Roosevelt*, p. 232; Rexford G. Tugwell, *The Democratic Roosevelt: A Biography of Franklin D. Roosevelt* (Garden City, N.Y.: Doubleday & Company, Inc., 1957), pp. 542-544.

19. *Public Papers and Addresses of Franklin D. Roosevelt. 1940 Volume*, pp. 483-485.

20. *Public Papers and Addresses of Franklin D. Roosevelt. 1940 Volume*, pp. 495-498.

21. *The New York Times*, October 19, 1940, p. 8.

22. William Allen White to Carl Sandburg, November 23, 1939. William Allen White Papers, Library of Congress; *The New York Times*, June 21, 1940, p. 19; June 20, 1940, p. 26.

23. Herbert Mitgang (ed.), *The Letters of Carl Sandburg* (New York: Harcourt Brace Jovanovich, Inc., 1968), p. 298; Carl Sandburg, "Lincoln–Roosevelt," *Today*, I (February 10, 1934), 5; Carl Sandburg to Franklin D. Roosevelt, March 29, 1935. Roosevelt Papers, PPF 4509; Carl Sandburg in "How They Are Voting: III," *The New Republic*, LXXXVIII (October 14, 1936), 277.

24. *The Sandburg Range: An Exhibit of Materials from Carl Sandburg's Library* (University of Illinois: Adah Patton Memorial Fund Publilication No. Six, 1958), p. 46.

25. Carl Sandburg, *Home Front Memo* (New York: Harcourt Brace Jovanovich, Inc., 1943), p. 30.

26. *New York Post*, November 5, 1940, p. 10.

27. Stephen Vincent Benét, *We Stand United and Other Radio Scripts* (New York: Farrar & Rinehart, 1945), pp. 4-6.

28. *Ibid.*, pp. 6-7.

29. *The New York Times*, November 7, 1940, p. 1.

30. Robert E. Sherwood, "To Whom It May Concern," *Good Housekeeping*, CVIII (February 1939), 17.

notes to chapter 6

1. Walter Johnson, *William Allen White's America* (New York: Henry Holt and Company, 1947), pp. 57, 425, 447, 466; William Allen White, *Forty Years on Main Street* (New York: Farrar & Rinehart, Inc., 1937), p. 120; *The New York Times*, July 21, 1937, p. 8.

2. David Hinshaw, *A Man from Kansas: The Story of William Allen White* (New York: G. P. Putnam's Sons, 1945), pp. 63, 72; Carl Sandburg to William Allen White, November 27, 1939. William Allen White Papers. Library of Congress; Johnson, *William Allen White's America*, p. 476.

3. White, *Forty Years on Main Street*, p. 211.

4. Walter Johnson, *The Battle Against Isolation* (Chicago: University of Chicago Press, 1944), pp. 47-48; Carl Sandburg to William Allen White, November 27, 1939. White Papers.

5. William Allen White (ed.), *Defense for America* (New York: The Macmillan Company, 1940), p. xiv.

6. White (ed.), *Defense for America*, pp. xv-xvi, xviii (italics added).

7. Johnson, *William Allen White's America*, p. 533.

8. Johnson, *The Battle Against Isolation*, p. 82.

9. *The Public Papers and Addresses of Franklin D. Roosevelt. 1940 Volume: War—and Aid to Democracies* (New York: Macmillan Company, 1941), pp. 263-264.

10. *The Public Papers and Addresses of Franklin D. Roosevelt. 1940 Volume*, pp. 640, 643.

11. *The New York Times*, December 30, 1940, p. 8; Johnson, *The Battle Against Isolation*, p. 192.

12. *The New York Times*, April 18, 1941, p. 8.

13. *The New York Times*, April 24, 1941, pp. 1, 12; Charles A. Lindbergh, "We Cannot Win This War for England," *Vital Speeches of the Day*, VII (May 1, 1941), 424-425.

14. Robert E. Sherwood, *Roosevelt and Hopkins: An Intimate History* (New York: Harper & Brothers, 1948), p. 153; *The New York Times*, April 26, 1941, pp. 1, 5; Samuel I. Roseman (ed.), *The Public Papers and Addresses of Franklin D. Roosevelt. 1941 Volume: The Call to Battle Stations* (New York: Harper & Brothers, 1940), pp. 137-138.

15. *Newsweek*, XVII (May 5, 1941), 18.

16. Carl Sandburg, *Home Front Memo* (New York: Harcourt Brace Jovanovich, Inc., 1943), p. 34.

17. *Ibid.*, pp. 72-74.

18. *Ibid.*, pp. 94-96.

19. *The New York Times*, September 12, 1941, p. 2.

20. *The New York Times*, September 13, 1941, p. 1.

21. Johnson, *William Allen White's America*, p. 554.

notes to chapter 7

1. Carl Sandburg, *Home Front Memo* (New York: Harcourt Brace Jovanovich, Inc.), n.p.

2. Stephen Vincent Benét, *Burning City: New Poems* (New York: Farrar & Rinehart, 1936), pp. 26-41.

3. Stephen Vincent Benét, *A Summons to the Free* (New York: Farrar & Rinehart, Inc., 1941), pp. 28-32.

4. *Ibid.*, pp. 8-12.

5. *Ibid.*, pp. 20-22.

6. Charles A. Fenton, *Stephen Vincent Benét: The Life and Times of an American Man of Letters, 1898-1943* (New Haven: Yale University Press, 1958), p. 363; *Life*, XI (July 7, 1941), 90-96.

7. Stephen Vincent Benét, *We Stand United and Other Radio Scripts* (New York: Farrar & Rinehart, Inc., 1945), pp. 141-154.

8. Sandburg, *Home Front Memo*, pp. 83-86, 114-117.

9. *There Were Giants in the Land* (New York: Farrar & Rinehart, Inc., 1942), p. 226.

10. *Ibid.*, pp. 229-232.

11. Gerald W. Johnson, *New York Herald Tribune Books*, XIX (September 13, 1942), 5.

12. Sandburg, *Home Front Memo*, p. 53.

13. *Ibid.*, pp. 33-35.
14. *Ibid.*, pp. 35-36.
15. *Ibid.*, pp. 52, 85, 98.
16. Samuel I. Rosenman, *Working with Roosevelt* (New York: Harper & Brothers, 1952), p. 275; Samuel I. Rosenman (ed.), *The Public Papers and Addresses of Franklin D. Roosevelt. 1941 Volume: The Call to Battle Stations* (New York: Harper & Brothers Publishers, 1950), p. 85.
17. Rosenman (ed.), *Public Papers and Addresses of Franklin D. Roosevelt. 1941 Volume*, p. 87.
18. *Ibid.*, p. 328.
19. *Ibid.*, p. 329.
20. *The New York Times*, August 20, 1941, p. 1; August 21, 1941, p. 16.
21. *Time*, XXXIX (January 5, 1942), 14-15.

notes to chapter 8

1. Thomas A. Bailey, *Presidential Greatness: The Image and the Man from George Washington to the Present* (New York: Appleton-Century, 1966), pp. 20-22.
2. Samuel I. Rosenman (ed.), *The Public Papers and Addresses of Franklin D. Roosevelt. 1944-45 Volume: Victory and the Threshold of Peace* (New York: Harper & Brothers, 1950), pp. 206, 354-355; Tamara K. Hareven, *Eleanor Roosevelt: An American Conscience* (Chicago: Quadrangle Books, 1968), p. 188.
3. William Allen White, "Emporia in Wartime," *The New Republic*, CVI (April 13, 1942), 492; Walter Johnson, *William Allen White's America* (New York: Henry Holt and Company, 1947), p. 563.
4. Stephen Vincent Benét, *America* (New York: Farrar and Rinehart, Inc., 1944), p. 76.
5. *Ibid.*, p. 112.
6. August Derleth, *The Chicago Sun Book Week*, I (September 26, 1943), 4.

INDEX

Abe Lincoln in Illinois (Sherwood), 5; background of play, 38–40; compared with *Prologue to Glory*, 40–41; summary of play, 40–41; contemporary lessons of play, 42–47; film version, 47–49; praised by Eleanor Roosevelt, 71–72

Abraham Lincoln: The Prairie Years (Sandburg), 34, 51, 75; interpretation of Lincoln, 31–32; compared with *John Brown's Body*, 33; compared with *Prologue to Glory*, 36; influence upon Sherwood, 38–39

Abraham Lincoln: The War Years (Sandburg), 50, 75, 103, 109; evolution of, 51–53; reception by reviewers, 53–55; interpretation of Lincoln, 55–59; overall significance of, 59–61; Roosevelt cites, 70–71, 109

Adams, Franklin P., 78

America (Benét), 115–116

America First, 80, 91, 92, 115

American Youth Congress, 70

Anderson, Maxwell, 39

Andrew Jackson (James), 24

Atkinson, Brooks, 36, 39

Atlantic Conference, 109

Basler, Roy P., 35

Beard, Charles A., 53–55

Becker, Carl L., 21

Benét, Stephen Vincent, 4, 5, 11, 21, 29, 35, 117; and Lincoln, 32–34, 79, 97, 99, 113, 115–116; and Whitman, 32, 103; review of *Abraham Lincoln: The War Years*, 53, 61–62; and Roosevelt, 78–80, 98, 107; and Sandburg, 97; propagandist for intervention, 97–103, 107. Works: *America*, 115–116; "Democracy is the Revolution," 100; *John Brown's Body*, 32–34, 75; "Listen to the People," 100–102; "Litany for Dictatorships," 98; "Nightmare at Noon," 98–99; "Ode to Walt Whitman," 98; "The Power of the Written Word," 99–100; "Tuesday, November 5th, 1940," 78–79; *Western Star*, 103

Benjamin Franklin (Van Doren), 21

Beveridge and the Progressive Era (Bowers), 21
Biography: "new," 11, 19, 31; changing trends in, 19-20; during 1930s, 20-22
Bourne, Randolph, 9
Bowers, Claude G., 27, 65
Brant, Irving, 28
Bromfield, Louis, 14
Brooks, Van Wyck, 8-11, 13, 14. Works: *Makers and Finders*, 20; *The Ordeal of Mark Twain*, 13, 20; *The Pilgrimage of Henry James*, 13; *The Wine of the Puritans*, 11
Brown, John Mason, 38

Canby, Henry Seidel, 21, 32
Chicago Poems (Sandburg), 30
Chicago Times, 103
Churchill, Winston S., 109
Clemens, Samuel L., [pseud. Mark Twain], 23-24
Clurman, Harold, 8, 42
Commager, Henry Steele, 53-55, 61
Committee to Defend America by Aiding the Allies, 5, 72, 87, 89, 91
Conkle, E. P., 35-37. Work: *Prologue to Glory*, 35-37, 40-41
Council for Democracy, 79
Course of American Democratic Thought, The (Gabriel), 63-64
Cowley, Malcolm, 15, 19
Crowder, Richard, 52
Curti, Merle, 8

Dallman, V. Y., 84
Davis, Elmer, 116
Defense for America (White), 86, 87
"Democracy is the Revolution" (Benét), 100
Democratic Party, 69, 82
Derleth, August, 117
DeVoto, Bernard, 11, 20, 24, 49

Dictionary of American Biography, The, 15-16
Dorsey, Frank, 69
Dos Passos, John, 13
Du Pont family, 69, 73
Early, Steve, 95
Elihu Root (Jessup), 21
Emporia Gazette (White), 82, 85, 91, 96
Expatriates of 1920s, 14-15

Flanagan, Hallie, 36, 37
Ford, Henry, 10, 33
Fox, Dixon Ryan, 16
Frank, Waldo, 9
Freeman, Douglas Southall, 21
Fuess, Claude, 11

Gabriel, Ralph Henry, 63-64, 65
Gone with the Wind (Mitchell), 19
Great Depression (1929-1939), 7, 8, 12, 25, 51, 78; and historical writing, 17-18; and biography, 19-20; parallel with secession crisis, 65

Hamilton, Alexander, 28; image of during 1920s, 25-27
Hero in America, The (Wecter), 64
Hibben, Paxton, 11
Hill, Henry Bartram, 53
Hinshaw, David, 84
History of American Life, The (Schlesinger and Fox), 15-16
Home Front Memo (Sandburg), 97, 117
Hoover, Herbert, 3, 10, 74, 84; on Lincoln and the New Deal, 68-69
Hopkins, Harry, 72
Hull, Cordell, 77, 85

Idiot's Delight (Sherwood), 45

Jackson, Andrew, 69; image of during 1930s, 23-24

James, Marquis, 24
Jefferson and Hamilton (Bowers), 26-27
Jefferson, Thomas, 69, 74; image of: during 1920s, 25, 26-27; during 1930s, 27-29; compared with Lincoln's 29
Jessup, Philip C., 21
John Brown's Body (Benét), 32, 33, 75; interpretation of Lincoln, 34
John D. Rockefeller (Nevins), 20
Johnson, Allen, 16
Johnson, Edgar, 21-22
Johnson, Gerald W., 105
Johnson, Lyndon B., 6

Kazin, Alfred, 8, 19, 24
Knox, Frank, 89

La Guardia, Fiorello, 70, 84
Leaves of Grass (Whitman), 102
Lee, Robert E., 33, 91
Lend-Lease, 90, 106
Lerner, Max, 54, 61, 68, 71
Lewis, Lloyd, 21, 35, 53, 62. Works: *Myths After Lincoln*, 35; *Sherman: Fighting Prophet*, 21
Liberty League, 28, 69, 80; attacked by Roosevelt, 73-74
Life, 48, 101
Life and Times of William Howard Taft, The (Pringle), 20
Life of Emerson, The (Brooks), 20
Lincoln, Abraham, 37, 72, 103, 106, 115; image of: during 1930s, 4, 23-24, 29, 49, 63-64; in Sandburg's work, 29-32; 53-59; 60-62; 97; in Benét's work, 32-34, 97; in Conkle's work, 35-37; in Sherwood's work, 39-49; turning point in the uses of, 80-81; during foreign policy debates, 96. Cited or quoted by: Roosevelt, 65-68, 70, 71,

73-74, 82, 108-110; Hoover, 68; Democratic Party, 69; Lerner, 71; Sandburg, 52, 77, 94, 104-106, 117; Benét, 79, 99, 116; Sherwood, 81, 113; White, 83-84, 86-88, 91; compared with Roosevelt, 4-6, 108, 112-114; by Sandburg, 76; by Benét, 98; compared with White, 83-85
Lincoln Legend, The (Basler), 35
"Lincoln—Roosevelt" (Sandburg), 76
Lindbergh, Charles A., 10, 83, 95; and White, 91-92, 95-96; and America First, 92-93; Sherwood on, 93; Roosevelt attacks, 93, 104; Sandburg attacks, 93-95
"Listen to the People" (Benét), 100-102
"Litany for Dictatorships" (Benét), 98
"Lost Generation," 14-15
Ludwig, Emil, 67-68

MacLeish, Archibald, 5
Main Currents in American Thought (Parrington), 15, 26
Makers and Finders (Brooks), 20
Mark Twain's America (DeVoto), 20
Massey, Raymond, 42, 45-46, 48, 75; quoted on Roosevelt, 43, 45; reads Benét statement, 79-80, 100
Masters, Edgar Lee, 11, 24
Mellon, Andrew, 26
Mencken, H. L., 10
Mitchell, Margaret, 19
Moley, Raymond, 68, 76
Morgenthau, Henry, Jr., 104-105
Morrison, Theodore, 100
Mumford, Lewis, 9
Mussolini, Benito, 88, 89
Myths After Lincoln (Lewis), 35

Neuberger, Richard L., 68

Nevins, Allan, 20, 21, 53-55, 61
New Deal, 7, 35, 38, 52, 70; and
 Lincoln, 4, 65, 67-68, 69, 82;
 and Hamilton, 28; and Jefferson, 28; Hoover on, 68-69;
 Benét on, 78, 98; White on
 84, 85
New York Herald Tribune Forum,
 74
New York Times, 80, 110
"Nightmare at Noon" (Benét),
 98-99
Non-Partisan Committee for Peace
 through revision of the Neutrality Law, 85

"Ode to Walt Whitman" (Benét),
 98
Office of War Information (OWI),
 115, 116
Oppenheim, James, 9
Ordeal of Mark Twain, The
 (Brooks), 13, 20

Parrington, Vernon Louis, 15, 26
People, Yes, The (Sandburg), 52,
 102
Perry, Ralph Barton, 21
Pilgrimage of Henry James, The
 (Brooks), 13
"Power of the Written Word,
 The" (Benét), 99-100
Pringle, Henry F., 20
Prologue to Glory (Conkle),
 35-37; compared with *Abe
 Lincoln in Illinois* 40-41

Randall, James G., 53-54
R. E. Lee (Freeman), 21
Republican Party, 83, 84
Rice, Elmer, 39, 41
Roosevelt, Eleanor (Mrs. Franklin
 D.), 71-72, 113
Roosevelt, Franklin D., 3, 7, 18,
 24, 28, 117; and Lincoln, 4-6,
 29, 64-71, 73-74, 82, 96,
 108-110, 112-114; and Jef-
 ferson, 26-28; and Sherwood,

42-44, 48-49, 71-75, 80,
 108; and Sandburg, 52, 68,
 75-78, 94, 104-105, 107;
 heroic proportions of, 64,
 111; 1940 campaign of,
 71-75; and Benét, 78-80, 98,
 107; and White, 83-85,
 87-91; Charlottesville speech,
 88-89; Lend-Lease speech,
 90-91; and Lindbergh, 93-95;
 Time man of the year, 1941,
 110-111
Roosevelt, Theodore, 66, 69, 74
Roseman, Samuel I., 72-73, 108

Sandburg, Carl, 4, 33, 35, 49, 80,
 116-117; and Lincoln, 5,
 29-32, 104-105, 113; and
 Whitman, 30, 57-59; and
 Sherwood, 39; and Roosevelt,
 52, 68, 75-78, 94, 104-105,
 107; and Benét, 53, 61-62,
 97; and White, 84, 86; and
 Lindbergh, 93-95; propagan-
 dist for intervention,
 103-107. Works: *Abraham
 Lincoln: The Prairie Years*,
 31-33, 36, 38-39, 51, 75;
 *Abraham Lincoln: The War
 Years*, 50, 51-61, 70, 75,
 103, 109; *Chicago Poems*, 30;
 Home Front Memo, 97, 117;
 "Lincoln–Roosevelt," 76;
 The People, Yes, 52, 102;
 Storm Over the Land, 62
Saturday Review of Literature, 44
Schlesinger, Arthur M., 16
Seven Arts, 9-10
Sherman: Fighting Prophet
 (Lewis), 21
Sherman, Stuart, 30
Sherwood, Robert E., 4, 38, 71,
 93, 117; and Lincoln, 5, 39,
 45-46, 49, 81 113; and
 Roosevelt, 42-44, 48-49,
 71-75, 80, 108; and Sand-
 burg, 54, 60; and White, 83,
 87; on Lindbergh, 93; and

Office of War Information, 116. Works: *Abe Lincoln in Illinois* (play), 5, 38-47; *Abe Lincoln in Illinois* (film), 47-49; *Idiot's Delight*, 45
Smith, Alfred E., 28
Stearns, Harold, 9, 14
Stimson, Henry L., 89
Storm Over the Land (Sandburg), 62

Theodore Roosevelt (Pringle), 20
There Were Giants in the Land, 105-106
Thomas, Parnell, 36-37
Thompson, Dorothy, 77
Thoreau (Canby), 21
Thought and Character of William James, The (Perry), 21
Time, 110-111
Tolstoy, Leo, 59
"Tuesday, November 5th, 1940" (Benét), 78-79
Tugwell, Rexford G., 73
Twain, Mark. See Clemens, Samuel L.

Usable past, search for a: before World War I, 8-10; during 1920s, 10-11, 14-16; after Great Crash, 12, 16-24; 1930s compared with prewar, 12-14, 16-17

Vallandigham, Clement, 93, 94, 104

Van Doren, Carl, 20-21

Washington, George, 63, 64, 65, 74
Wecter, Dixon, 64
Western Star (Benét), 103
White, William Allen, 5, 85, 115; and Committee to Defend America by Aiding the Allies, 5, 87, 89, 91; and Sandburg, 75, 84, 86; and Lincoln, 82, 83-85, 86-88, 116; and Roosevelt, 83-85, 87-91; and Sherwood, 83, 87; on New Deal, 84, 85; internationalist activities of, 85-90; and Lindbergh, 91-92, 95-96. Work: *Defense for America*, 86-87
Whitman, Walt, 8-9, 23-24; Sandburg and, 30, 57-59; Benét and, 32, 98, 102, 103
Willkie, Wendell, 74-75, 89-90
Wine of the Puritans, The (Brooks), 11
WPA Federal Theatre, 35, 36-37
Woollcott, Alexander, 77

Young America, 9. *See also* Young Intellectuals, Young Radicals
Young Intellectuals, 8, 10, 12, 13. *See also* Young America, Young Radicals
Young Radicals, 17. *See also* Young America, Young Intellectuals